eBay Money Machine

5 Moves You Need to Make to Sell More Stuff on eBay

Copyright © 2014 / 2017 Nick Vulich

Copyright © 2017 Nick Vulich
All rights reserved.
ISBN: 9781546533511

(Author's Note:

*This book was originally published as **eBay 2015**. The shipping and bookkeeping sections eventually spun off into their own books. Now it's back and newly revised and updated as **eBay Money Machine**. Some readers are bound to ask, "why reprise a past work?" Or, "If it's already been published as three separate books—Is there any reason for another go-around?"*

That's a good question, and my answer simply is—Good Information Rises to the Top. It will help new sellers push their way upward and make more money with less time spent spinning their wheels. New sellers can benefit, too, by gaining a new perspective on their day to day tasks.

If I'm wrong—Amazon gives you seven days to get your money back—No Questions Asked.)

Table of Contents

Table of Contents 4
Getting Started 6
Why listen to me? 9
$10,000 a Month Selling on eBay... 12
Why you should sell on eBay & Amazon.............................. 14
The least you need to know 18
Getting Started on eBay.. 21
Make These Changes First.. 27
Plan for Success... 34
Uncover Your Niche 44
Ship Like a Pro 52
    Package Your Items Like a Pro 57
    Set Up Your Shipping Station 58
    Must Have Supplies 60
    Packaging Tips... 63
    Do I Need to Offer Free Shipping?............................ 67
    Setting Shipping Rates in eBay................................. 70
    Printing Shipping Labels Using eBay & PayPal 74
    Do I Need Insurance?.. 77
    Using a Third-Party Shipping Provider 80
Sell International 86
    eBay Global Shipping Program 89
    Enable Items for International Shipping 92
    List Your Items on International Sites...................... 97
    Open an International eBay Store 103

- Interview with Joseph Dattilo on International Shipping 105
  - Customs Forms 110
- Know Your Numbers 114
  - GoDaddy Bookkeeping 121
  - Keep Records the Old-fashioned Way 130
  - What You Need to Know About Taxes................... 133
  - Most Common Tax Deductions............................... 139
  - Business Permits, Licenses, and Such 143
  - Choose Your Business Structure 145
- Sell your Stuff Off eBay 149
  - Sell it on Amazon 151
  - Sell it on Etsy 164
  - Sell it on Fiverr 174

Getting Started

Selling on eBay isn't easy. It isn't for everyone. More than that, there is no guarantee you will make money at it.

Why am I telling you this? Because no one else will. Other authors are afraid you won't buy their book if no one is buying anything from you. I'm not going to lie to you.

It sucks, but...

If you are already selling on eBay, the odds are you are already feeling the pain. If you are new to eBay and are reading this book for advice on how to get started, keep in mind—selling on eBay doesn't mean you won't hit some icy patches now and then.

Most books that talk about how to sell online paint this rosy picture that tells potential sellers once you post your items for sale on eBay, you can spend the rest of your time lying around the house in your jammies or undies watching TV while the money rolls into your PayPal account 24 / 7.

I wish I could tell you that's the way it works, but that would be a bit like tossing you under the bus.

I will tell you that after you've been selling on eBay for a while it gets easier. You will make more sales, and many buyers will return to buy from you over and over again—if you give them good value for their money and great customer service.

Just keep in mind—it's a roller coaster ride, no matter how long you've been selling on eBay. Sales vary from season to season. Normally, the summer months—June, July and August are the slowest times, the Christmas season—November, Deceber and January is traditionally the strongest selling period. Many eBay sellers earn fifty to seventy-five percent of their profit during the holiday season. Where your sales fall on the scale depends upon the types of products you sell.

Ideally, you'll be able to develop a product mix that helps balance sales out, so you don't experience extreme seasonal fluctuations. It won't happen magically, though. It's something you will have to plan for and work into your marketing mix.

Sometimes, you will have a situation where you have been selling the same product for five or ten years, and all of a sudden sales stop and the market goes dead for what you are selling. When this occurs, you need to assess the situation quickly and determine what happened. Did a new competitor come into the marketplace and undercut your prices? Was a new product released that makes yours obsolete? Are too many sellers offering the same products that you are selling?

Whatever you do, you need to react quickly? Otherwise, it's like beating a dead horse. You will never get anywhere.

Hopefully, you've got a Plan B. And, that is what this book is all about. I am going to teach you about how to sell on eBay today— and tomorrow. To do that successfully you need to be able to move from Point A to Point B without tripping over your own feet.

Keep in mind that nothing I am going to tell you is new, nor should it come as a surprise to experienced sellers. This book isn't going to walk you through listing your items on eBay. There are plenty of books that do a great job of that.

You should also know, I haven't discovered any hidden secrets. Selling on eBay isn't rocket science. It takes a lot of hard work and some good old common sense.

If you can execute in five key areas, you'll have everything you need to succeed in online selling—today, tomorrow, and into the future.

1. Plan for success
2. Establish a Niche
3. Ship like a pro
4. Sell international
5. Know your numbers

Why listen to me?

Hey there, Nick Vulich here.

If you are like me, I'm sure you are probably a little skeptical about taking advice from someone without knowing a little bit about them first.

I have been selling on eBay since 1999. Most of my online customers know me as history-bytes, although I have also operated as its old news, back door video, and sports card one.

I have sold 30,004 items for a total of $411,755.44 over the past fifteen years, and that's just on my history-bytes id. Right now I have cut way back on eBay selling to focus on my writing, but I still keep my hat in the game. That way I can stay current with the challenges my readers face every day when they go to sell on eBay.

I have been an eBay Power Seller or Top-Rated Seller for most of the past fifteen years, which means I have met eBay's sales and customer satisfaction goals.

This book was originally published as *eBay 2015*. The shipping and bookkeeping sections eventually spun off into their own books. Now it's back and newly revised and updated as *eBay Money Machine*. Some readers are bound to ask, "Why reprise a past work?" Or, "If it's already been published as three separate books—Is there any reason for another?"

That's a good question, and my answer simply is—Good Information Rises to the Top. It will help new sellers push their way upwards and make more money with less time spent spinning their wheels. New sellers can benefit, too, by gaining a new perspective on their day to day tasks.

If I'm wrong—Amazon gives you seven days to get your money back—No Questions Asked.

This is the eighth book I've written about selling on eBay. The first two, *Freaking Idiots Guide to Selling on eBay*, and *eBay Unleashed*, are aimed more towards how to get started selling on eBay. *eBay 2014* is directed at more advanced sellers and tackles many of the challenges top-rated sellers face in the eBay marketplace. *eBay Subject Matter Expert* suggests a different approach to selling on eBay – building a platform where customers recognize you as an expert in your niche, and buy from you because of your knowledge in that field. *Sell It Online* gives a brief overview of selling on eBay, Amazon, Etsy, and Fiver. *How to Make Money Selling Old Books & Magazines on eBay* talks specifically about what I know best, how to sell books and magazines on eBay. *eBay Bookkeeping Made Easy* helps sellers understand how to keep track of the money they are making, and how to take advantage of the tax code to make even more money.

eBay 2015 is an attempt to tie it all together. For those of you who have been following along and reading all of my books, some of this is going to be a rehash. The section on bookkeeping is taken directly from my book *eBay Bookkeeping Made Easy*. It's not the entire book, but enough to give you a good primer on what it's going to take to run an eBay business. Some of the materials in the sections on shipping and international selling are excerpted from my book *eBay Shipping Simplified*. Again, it's info you need to know and apply today to thrive on eBay.

My goal is to help you become as successful as you wish to be. **Let's get started.**

$10,000 a Month Selling on eBay

Sounds impossible, doesn't it?

I'm here to tell you, I have done it—and, so have thousands of other sellers.

You can too!

It's just a matter of getting started.

I have new sellers ask me every day, "What's the secret to selling on eBay?" or "What's the best way to get started selling on Amazon?"

Here's what I tell, them, and what I'm going to tell you.

"Get started. "

List your first item today. Don't worry about what you don't know, or what you think you need to know.

"Just do it!"

It really is that simple. I can tell you everything I know about how to sell on eBay. I can tell you what products to sell. I can tell you how much to charge, and what type of listing template to use. I can tell you the best time to start and end your listings, and how to ship your items, and on—and on.

But, there's one thing I can't do.

I can't make you get started.

Think about that for a moment. Every day hundreds of people buy guides just like this one. They read them from cover to cover. Many of them underline important passages and scribble notes in the margins, or on a notepad.

They plan what they're going to do; what they're going to sell; and how much money they are going to make.

And, then...they begin to doubt themselves. They ask themselves questions—like what if it doesn't work? What if I list my items wrong? What if my items don't sell? What will I tell my friends if I fail?

Does any of this sound familiar?

What I'm trying to help you understand here is simple. We are all plagued by self-doubt. Everybody questions things when they are first getting started with something new. What you need to do if you want to become successful is to overcome these doubts.

It's like learning to walk. You put one foot in front of the other and keep moving. If you fall down—you dust yourself off and keep moving.

Selling online is like learning to walk.

You try one product or one listing. If your item doesn't sell, you find another one, and try again. If your item sells, you tweak your description or product so that you can sell even more.

If you don't learn anything else from reading this book, keep this one bit of information in the back of your mind.

Success is all about getting started.

Why you should sell on eBay & Amazon

eBay and Amazon are two of the largest e-commerce websites in the world. Together, they account for over $150 billion dollars in sales every year. They have nearly 400 million registered users.

And, the best part is—they let you tap into their user base to sell your products and services.

For the average person who wants to start an online business, eBay and Amazon are the easiest way to get started. Just list your item on their website, and they make it available to more than 400 million ready buyers. You don't need to do anything else. There's no SEO, no blogging, or costly PPC ads on Google or Facebook.

All you need to do is list your item on eBay or Amazon, and you're in business.

If you're new to online selling—eBay and Amazon are a great way to cut your teeth in e-commerce.

Of the two sites, Amazon makes getting started the easiest. I liken it to hitchhiking on someone else's business. All you do is look for a listing similar to what you want to sell, and select the <sell on Amazon> button next to where it says, "Have one to sell?" After that, you follow the prompts—add your item condition, asking price, and walla, your item is for sale on Amazon.

It really is that simple.

Of course, not every item you run across is going to be available for sale on Amazon. Sometimes you stumble across a new or unique item no one has listed for sale yet. Not a problem. Amazon has a tool that lets you create a new listing page for it. We'll talk more about using it later in this guide.

Amazon also has a few restrictions on products you can sell, especially around Christmas and other big holidays. They don't want the little guys selling against them or their big merchants in these product lines. It's just one of those things you need to deal with. Most times, when I bump into one of these categories Amazon shows me that my listing has been blocked. Translation: it's not being shown to visitors on the Amazon website. It's still there, but only Amazon and I can see it.

eBay offers a similar feature. Under the pictures, at the top of the item listing page, you'll see the words, "Have one to sell?" Next, to that, you'll see some blue text that says <Sell now>. Select that, and it will bring up an item description page pre-populated with many of the item details you need to list the item.

It's not quite as simple to use as Amazon's piggybacking feature, but with a few tweaks, you can produce a great looking listing page. eBay requires you to add at least one picture of the product you are trying to sell. You can also change the description a bit to better fit what you are selling, maybe talk about the color, any accessories you are including, and add a little detail describing any of the rough spots. Doing this helps potential buyers get a better feel for the item you are selling.

And, just like Amazon, eBay lets you add new listing pages from scratch when you have an item that is unique to the website. We will go further into that in another chapter. For now, just keep in mind—eBay and Amazon give you lots of flexibility in how you list and sell your items. The exact listing method you decide to use should be dictated by the item you are selling, the venue you choose to list it on, and what your individual sales goals are.

Which site should you sell on?

Often, your products will sell equally well on eBay or Amazon. Other times, one site is better suited to what you are selling.

How do you decide which site is the best for what you want to sell?

eBay is better suited for selling unique, higher priced items, or items you are unsure about the value of. If you have multiples of an item, eBay's auction feature allows you to experiment and test the waters. Auctions also give you a chance to get a higher price for items you are unsure of the value of or items that have no set price. If you are nervous about not getting the right price for the item you are selling, you can set a reserve price. If your item doesn't reach the reserve price, it doesn't sell.

Use Amazon to list everyday items—books, textbooks, clothes, shoes, cell phones, and other electronics. Just about anything that is a consistent seller, and sells within a set price range is the perfect item for selling on Amazon.

Amazon's fee structure is close to eBay's. Final value fees are slightly higher, but they include payment processing fees. (On eBay, you need to make an extra payout to PayPal for credit card processing.) Amazon doesn't charge listing fees. They only get paid if your item sells.

Amazon also makes it easy to determine how quickly your items should sell. Amazon ranks every item based on how well it sells. Let's look at books as an example. There are millions of books listed for sale on Amazon. Each one has a product ranking from one to blah-blah million. The lower the ranking of the book, the better the sales of the book. Books ranked under 100 are super-fast sellers; books ranked under 10,000 are consistently good sellers, and books ranked under 50,000 are still selling several copies per week.

Once you are familiar with Amazon's ranking system, it makes it easy to pick consistent winners.

To discover the best sellers on eBay takes a little more work. By employing eBay's advanced search feature, you can see how many of each item sold recently, and how much they sold for. By consistently using this information to source product you can pick better selling merchandise to list.

The least you need to know

Traditionally, eBay releases two seller-updates every year—one in the spring, and another in the fall. These updates are eBay's way of giving seller's a heads-up to let them know what's coming down the pipeline and the changes they need to prepare for.

Here's a quick run-down of what sellers can expect from the 2016 Fall Seller Update.

- Active content is prohibited from the site beginning in June of 2016. That means no more videos or animations are allowed in auction listings.
- Performance standards are changing. Buyer feedback, DSRs, and other incidents that get resolved successfully (with your buyer) will no longer count against you. eBay says they're going to concentrate on what matters most.
- Return policies have been tweaked. Beginning in October of 2016, sellers will have the option to exchange or replace items, rather than to just give refunds.

- Turbo Lister is being phased out in June of 2017. Many of its features will be incorporated into the new seller hub.
- Finally, category updates are ongoing. As eBay continues its move to be more like Amazon, sellers will need to update listings to add category specific information.

Overall, the changes reflect a more focused eBay. They are looking at the new online marketplace and making changes to ensure the site stays relavant to shoppers. That's good news for everyone. Buyers will find more items they want, need, and are willing to spend their money on, and sellers will hear the jingle where it counts—in their pocketbook.

The 2016 Spring Seller Update hit many sellers where it hurts - in the pocketbook. eBay store prices took a hefty jump, in return for a larger allotment of free listings.

Basic store prices jumped to $24.95; **Premium** stores moved to $74.95, and **Anchor** stores increased over 75 percent to $349.95. For high volume sellers, the new price structure should come as a welcome change. For most eBayers, the *2016 Spring Seller Update* means they will pay a higher price to play.

- eBay decided mobile is where sales are moving. They announced the end of active content in listings beginning in June of 2017 to provide mobile users a better experience. eBay also created a new view item feature for mobile. It displays a 250-character text-only description to mobile users. The idea is to provide relevant details—quickly, for time conscious mobile shoppers.

- In a move to be more like Amazon, eBay is expanding product reviews to more categories and products. Their research shows product reviews keep buyers on the site longer and increase sales as much as 18 percent.

Again, the updates come from a milder, but still money-grubbing eBay. While Amazon, and other online retailers, make their money on the backend, eBay continues to take their cut on both ends of the transaction.

That's not a problem—if they can draw more active buyers to the site. Until they do that, eBay needs to get its house in order.

Getting Started on eBay

Pretty near every writer begins their spiel about selling on eBay by talking about what to sell or how to sell, but they are all missing the most important element to continued success selling on eBay—building a strong reputation. If you don't have awesome feedback, it's going to be tough to grow your sales.

If you are unfamiliar with buying and selling on eBay, buyers and sellers rate each other based on a five-star rating system. The system is somewhat skewed towards the buyer because if they are unhappy they can leave negative feedback for the seller. Sellers can no longer leave negative feedback for buyers.

Buyers look at your feedback rating to determine whether it's safe to purchase an item from you. If two sellers are offering the same item for close to the same price, buyers will make their purchase from the seller who has better feedback. It just makes sense to spend your money with someone who has a good reputation.

As a result, your number one goal is to ensure customers are delighted with their purchases and leave you great feedback. Sounds easy, doesn't it? Let's look at a couple of examples that can cause the buyer to leave negative feedback.

- When customers make a purchase, eBay shows buyers an estimated delivery time. Top-rated sellers are required to ship their items within 24 hours, which means they're doing their part to ensure the item delivers on time. Many times—the post office delivers packages outside of eBay's estimated delivery time. When this happens disgruntled buyers sometimes leave sellers negative feedback, even though the late delivery has nothing to do with them.
- Sometimes purchasers suffer from buyer's remorse and change their mind before the seller ships the item. Before September 20th, 2014 that wasn't a big problem. The seller could send in a request to cancel the sale, and when the buyer accepted it, everything was ok. The reality today with eBay grading sellers on the defect system means when a buyer changes their mind they are putting the seller on the spot. The seller is forced to choose between offering good customer service and canceling the sale, or telling the customer, "Sorry you're going to have to contact eBay to do that." The reason is when the buyer makes the request to cancel; the seller doesn't get charged with a defect. But, wait—there's a massive "Catch 22" lurking here. If the seller waits for the cancellation to go through eBay, the odds are he's going to be late with his agreed upon shipping time. That's a seller defect. Too many of them and you could get tossed off eBay.
- Here's another situation you may find yourself embroiled in. Many times, customers make a purchase and ask the seller to hold off mailing the item until they return from vacation, or until it's closer to the recipient's birthday. Good customer

service says you should hold the item for the specified period, but if you do—eBay looks at it as a seller defect.

These are some of the situations you're going find yourself up against trying to offer good customer service, while at the same time trying to maintain a low defect rate with eBay. I can't tell you how to deal with these issues. It's something you're going to have to work out on a case-by-case basis.

That's a quick overview of customer service.

Selling on eBay is all about creating product listings that get customers excited about what you're selling.

When you create your listings, you need to...

Create a title loaded with keywords.

eBay gives you 80 characters to describe what you're selling. Make them count.

Here's a secret many sellers don't know or understand. Your title contains the search terms for what you are selling. It's how buyers find what you are selling amongst the millions of other things for sale on eBay.

Don't waste words. Make every keyword you include in your title count. The easiest way to do this is to think about how you would search for that item. What words would you use? What are the most important things you are looking for? Some of the obvious choices are—manufacturer, model number, color, condition—new, used, and refurbished free shipping, and easy returns.

Take large. Well-lit photos.

Selling online is all about the pictures. Every day the internet is becoming more of a visual experience. Think about social media. The most shared posts today are short videos, cat pictures, pictures of adults and children acting stupid, and those cutesy illustrations with quotes attached to them.

What does that mean for online sellers?

You need to include large clear pictures in all your listings. They need to show the item you are selling from different angles. If the item you are selling has any damage, you need to include close-up pictures of the affected areas.

Your pictures should be so clear your customer feels they can reach out and touch what you are selling. A cover designer on Fiverr explained this better than I ever could. She said the chocolate shown on her covers is so realistic you will want to lick it.

Make all your pictures that good and you will make more money than ever before.

Write a benefit driven description.

Most sellers, recite all the droll facts that describe what they are selling. "I have a yellow taxi cab from 1964. It has an AM radio, bald tires, a spare tire, and oh yeah—it only runs when you can get a few friends together to give it a push." Slightly humorous, but dull. It doesn't contain anything that compels you to buy the yellow taxi.

You need to create listings that mimic the way people read on the internet. Most people read the headlines and then skim through the copy looking for details that interest them. If you list your key points using bullet points your customer's eyes are going to move directly from the headlines to the bullet points.

Another mistake sellers make is rambling off a slew of features. Customers could care less about features. They want to know what's in it for them.

Tell them the benefits.

- Your new TV comes equipped with a full-featured remote, so you never need to get out of your chair to change the channel or adjust the volume.
- Your new theater chairs are awesome. They have a built-in refrigerator and urination control system, so you never miss a moment of programming to grab another beer or go number one.

Research your item, and price it to sell.

Inexperienced sellers rush to post their listings for sale and settle for whatever price they get. Successful online sellers research every item before they post their listing. That way they know how likely it is to sell, how much money they can reasonably expect to get for it, and what the best keywords are to include in their title and listing description.

They know that the more time and research they put into selling an item the more money, they're going to make.

Manage buyer expectations.

Describe your item—warts and all.

Making a successful sale online or in person is all about managing buyer expectations. Your listing needs to get buyers excited about what you are selling. You need to make them visualize your item, and picture how much fun they are going to have using it. But, before you go in for the kill, you need to make them pull back for a moment. List any defects or blemishes your item has. If you are selling a cell phone, be sure to tell potential buyers which carriers it is and is not compatible with.

Many sellers are afraid to mention problems or defects because they think it will kill the sale. A lot of times it does just the opposite. When you take time out to explain defects and any potential problems they may encounter buyers are more likely to feel they can trust you.

Make These Changes First

From my experience selling on eBay, there are certain actions sellers can take that will increase their chances of being more successful.

If you are a seller teetering on the brink of success instituting some of these changes could give you the extra nudge you have been looking for to break into the big time. If you are a new seller, there's no better time to get started doing things the right way. You don't have any nasty habits to break. Just jump in and get started.

Keep in mind—this is stuff that has worked for me with the items I sell. Not everything will work for you. Keep doing what works for you—adjust, or discard the rest.

1. Remove all HTML code from your listings.

eBay's Cassini Search does not play well with HTML code—especially when you have HTML code in the listing header.

I love a fancy listing template with a great design and perfectly formatted pictures, but what I like even better is listening to the cash register ding on my eBay app.

If your sales are down, and nothing you do is working—strip the header out of a few listings, strip all of that fancy formatting and templates out of a few more. Then see what happens.

If unformatted listings allow you to make more sales, that's the way to go. By doing this, you can decide for yourself what works and what doesn't.

2. After you post a listing check it out on your smartphone and tablet. If you have trouble viewing your listing, re-work it, or cancel the listing and start over.

The internet today is all about mobile. People constantly check their phones, tablets, and Kindles all day long for new emails, tweets, and Facebook updates. Last Christmas, over fifty percent of holiday shopping took place on mobile devices. This year that number is expected to be closer to sixty percent.

If you don't optimize your listings for mobile, you are going to miss out on over half the customers who search for your items.

At the end of the day when you finish listing items, check some of your listings with your smartphone or iPad. Ensure your items appear in search, and that you optimize them for mobile viewing. If you inserted your photos into your listing using HTML code or a listing application like Auctiva or Ink Frog your pictures are going to appear small and they will be hard to view. If you posted them using eBay's *list your item page* your pictures expand to fill the entire device screen so that potential buyers will be able to use the arrow keys to move between one picture and another.

Ask yourself which format you are more likely to buy from and make the appropriate changes.

3. Get straight to the point. Less is better. People are in a hurry to get things done. The easier you make it to buy from you, the more stuff you're going to sell.

People are lazy. They read auction descriptions the same way they read blog posts and everything else on the internet. They scan the description for words that catch their fancy. They cruise through bullet points for a quick overview. They glance at the captions for pictures.

If they run into a big blob of text, they are going to click the back-arrow button and move on to the next listing. White space, bullet points, and bold headings are your allies in making more sales.

4. Include more and better pictures.

A good fifty percent of buyers make their decision just by looking at the pictures in your listing. They don't have time to read, or they don't want to read your item description. Many foreign buyers can't read or understand your description. They rely solely on the pictures you include to make their decision.

Some sellers play to this. They include lots of close-up pictures and encourage buyers to check the pictures and decide for themselves if the item meets their needs.

5. Focus on the 80/20 rule. Concentrate on selling the 20% of items that bring you the most profit. Scrap the slow sellers.

If you are like most sellers, a few of your items account for most of your sales volume.

If you have an eBay store, the odds are you have hundreds, maybe thousands of items languishing in there. Maybe ten or twenty sell every month, but the rest of them just sit there—festering. They suck up your monthly free listings and cost you additional listing fees. They taunt you into working extra hours hoping they will be that one extra sale you need to buy a new iPhone or an extra appetizer at lunch.

Quit playing the longshots. Take aim, and start focusing on sure things. Concentrate on the twenty percent of items that sell the best, don't waste time and money on listings that rarely sell.

6. Don't try to reinvent the wheel. It's great to find a new product that no one else has and will sell like hotcakes. There are very few items like that. If you focus all your time on looking for the newest greatest item you're going to miss out on a lot of sure things.

Everyone wishes they could go back in time and be the first guy in on the Hula Hoop craze, the Pet Rock, or the Chia Pet, but—those kinds of things are a one in a million shot. If you concentrate all your effort on the long ball, you're going to miss the sure hits along the way.

Sure—catching the wave on a new fad can make you rich and famous, but selling sure things like denim jackets, vintage toys, etc. will keep the cash registers ringing day in and day out. They'll put food on the table, and gas in your tank.

Chasing fads will suck up listing fees, the time you could spend posting profitable items, and free time you could have invested with your family and friends.

7. Don't beat a dead horse. Items run out of gas. They stop selling for one reason or another. Know when to call it quits and move on to a new niche.

Good things come to an end.

I've spent the last fifteen years selling vintage magazine articles, prints, and advertisements. They've been slugging along in low gear since the recession of 2008. eBay's move to fixed price listings is another nail in their coffin. Sales are down, selling prices are down, and profits are down.

I'm beating a dead horse.

I've got two choices—reinvent myself, or reimagine my product line. It's hard. We've been together for fifteen years. There's still money coming in—sometimes thousands of dollars a month, but it's nothing like it was.

The challenge for 2017 is to reinvent my business and carve out a new niche.

What about you? If you're beating a dead horse, do you have a plan to put it down, or breathe new life into it?

8. Spend more time on customer follow up. Chit chat. Shoot the shit. It's going to help you build a relationship with customers, and sell more stuff.

Getting to know your customers doesn't take that long. You just need to make it a regular part of your business day. When someone inquires about an item you have for sale—answer their question. Take a few minutes to thank them for contacting you. Talk up your item, and your product line. Ask how they're going to use it, and what other items they'd like to see you offer.

If it's close to a holiday—wish them a "Merry Christmas!" or a "Happy Easter!" If you want to be politically correct, wish them a "happy holiday season." Getting to know your customers only takes a few moments, but it gives buyers a warm and fuzzy feeling about doing business with you.

9. Try new things. Complacency has killed more businesses than anything else. Try selling at least one new product every week. At

the end of the year, if only five of them work, you've still got a stronger product line.

Products and entire product lines go stale. Things become obsolete. People become obsolete if they don't change. Think back to the guys you knew in high school and college. How many of them are still reliving their glory days? It's great to spend five or ten minutes with them and reminisce, but then you start to get this queasy feeling—this guy's not going anywhere. He's stuck in the past.

Products are the same as people. They get stuck in a certain period.

If you're not selling nostalgia, you need to cut the strings and try new things. It will make your product line stronger, and force you to become a better seller.

10. When a buyer protection case gets filed against you, put aside any personal feelings, or any thoughts you may have that the customer is trying to put one over on you. Pull the trigger. Give them a full refund—especially with low dollar amount items. You will feel better, and it will make you look better with your customers and with eBay.

Think of it this way. In the larger scheme of things—what's twenty, fifty, even a hundred dollars compared to everything you sell on eBay? You may be in the right. The customer may be taking advantage of you, but—is it worth lowering your ranking in search, or having your selling privileges restricted or revoked?

Probably not.

Look at the big picture, and do what's right for your business. Don't let personal feelings knock you down.

11. Take some extra time off—just for the heck of it. Selling on eBay is demanding. Customers are after you 24 / 7. You're rushing to list new items, and ship old ones before your 24-hour deadline expires. Take a break now and then to make time for yourself.

Selling on eBay is a tough racket. It never stops. There's always one more item to list, one more package to mail, and one more email to answer.

It will tear the hell out of you if you let it, and make you old before your time.

Be sure to schedule some time for yourself before you become the ogre in your basement dungeon.

12. Sell for charity.

eBay Giving Works makes it easy to sell for charity. Pick a national charity like the Red Cross, or pick a local charity that's close to your heart.

Add two or three charity auctions to your repertoire every month. It will make you feel better about selling on eBay. It will make your customers feel better about buying from you, and it will make you more money.

Not every charity Giving Works listing sells or sells for a higher price, but they do get a lot of page views. My normal listings receive twenty to twenty-five page views. When I add a charity to the listing, it draws several hundred page views, especially when I list using a large national charity.

Even when the item doesn't sell, that's a lot of extra eyes on my listings. Many of those lookers take a peek through my eBay store; some of them are likely to pick up an item or two while they look.

If you haven't tried it yet, list a couple of your items with eBay Giving Works. It just might become a habit.

Plan for Success

Too many sellers rush into eBay without a plan.

They jump in and start selling before they understand what the market is all about. Other newbies are sloppy. They post poorly lit pictures or write vague descriptions that don't tell buyers anything about what they are selling. Too often, sellers overprice or underprice items in their haste to get their listings posted. If they overprice their item, it doesn't sell, and they decide eBay doesn't work. It's just another scam that stole their money. If they underprice their item, and it sells, they complain because they can't make any money.

....

Selling on eBay is part art and part science.

I can teach you the science or the mechanics of selling on eBay, but to be successful; you need to understand the art of selling on eBay, or what I call gut instincts.

When you are scouting inventory, you need to be able to walk into a room and instantly zero in on the money items.

I sell books, magazines, and paper memorabilia. When I hit an estate sale, on my first round through the house that's all I look for.

The first thing I check for is vintage magazines. I've got a mental list of about twenty-five titles I always buy, but what excites me is when I come across something new; something I've never seen before; the more pictures they have in them, the more I want them.

I'm also scanning the room for items I don't normally sell, but things I think would complement my product line. Here's the way I look at it. If you see something totally new and unique that appeals to you, it's going to have that same effect on buyers in your niche.

I think Mike on *American Picker's* put it best, "In my business if you come across something you've never seen before the best time to buy it is now."

If you don't have that gut instinct to recognize something good—it's going to be harder to be successful on eBay.

Here's why?

If you don't have that gut instinct to recognize what's good and what's not, it's going to be like walking into a room with blinders on. There may be fifty items that will allow you to double or triple your money, but you could miss every single one of them because you're laser focused on just a few items you are comfortable selling.

That's good for the guy behind you. He's going to grab everything you walked by, and he's going to be able to pay his bills this week.

But it sucks for you.

You are going to be right back to thinking eBay is a scam, and there is no way anyone's making any money on the site. It happens every day. Don't believe me? Just hop on any eBay forum and get a whiff all of the bitching and whining. Need a little more convincing? Stop by the *Ecommerce-Bytes Blog* and check out some of the comments for any of their eBay related articles. It's the same people—constantly whining about how horrible and mean eBay is, and how they can't make a dime anymore because of that old Scrooge-like Mr. Donahue or his successors.

Guess what?

It's not eBay. It's you. It's your attitude.

The sooner you understand that whether you make or lose money on eBay is all about you and how you approach selling, the sooner you will find the success you want.

Let me tell you a story.

I used to be a salesman. I covered a four-state area (Iowa, Illinois, Missouri, and Wisconsin) for more years than I care to remember. Most of the time I did this I also sold historical memorabilia and sports cards on eBay. I popped listings up in between trips and phone calls, and I wasn't doing half bad. Most months I made $1500 to $2000 profit, $5 to $10 at a time.

One day I received a call from the VP of sales saying that the company had eliminated my position—but not to worry. They offered me a severance package, they agreed not to contest my unemployment, and they gave me a good reference. Of course, they did need one small favor in return—I had to sign a paper promising not to sue them for any of this.

What do you do?

If you want the money, you have to sign. To make a long story short, I signed the papers. I put work behind me and decided I was going to make a serious run at eBay.

If you tuned me out for reminiscing, here's where you might want to start listening again.

I decided to make a serious run at selling on eBay.

By most standards, I was already making good money. Fifteen hundred to two thousand dollars a month isn't chump change. The thing is: If I was going to make my living on eBay, I needed to double or triple that number before my unemployment and severance pay ran out. That gave me roughly six months to go from so-so to oh-boy.

To do that required some serious planning.

Making a Plan

Anybody can make a few sales on eBay. The key to success is to keep those sales growing while at the same time discovering new products to sell and new avenues to make your offerings available through.

Doing this isn't as easy as it sounds.

To be successful selling on eBay, or anywhere else for that matter, you need to have a plan, and you need to work your plan.

For me, one of the hardest parts of making a plan was already filled in. I knew what I wanted to sell—historical memorabilia and collectibles.

So, I knew the what.

I also knew the where. I wanted to sell my items on eBay.

That left the who, the why, and the how. If I planned on being successful, I needed to connect all of the dots.

That meant answering the who's.

1. Who are my customers?
2. Who is my competition?

I needed to answer the why's.

1. Why do customers buy the stuff I sell?
2. Why should these customers buy from me, instead of from another eBay store?

I also had to understand the how's.

1. How do I list my items for maximum impact?
2. How am I going to ship my items—both economically and safely?
3. How am I going to find a steady supply of products to sell so I can keep my business growing?

To put together an effective business plan, you need to answer all of the above questions.

I was lucky. I already knew what I wanted to sell. A lot of sellers who are new to eBay stumble when asked that question. For many new sellers, uncertainty about what to sell is the major stumbling block that keeps them from becoming successful.

I'm going to cover that topic in much more detail in the section about how to discover your niche. For now, we're going to concentrate on answering the other questions posed above.

Who are my customers, and why should they buy from me

If you're already selling on eBay, it's going to be much easier to answer these questions. The best way to do this is to ask your customers directly. Every time you send out a customer service email, include a brief survey.

It can be as simple as,

Thanks again for making your purchase from history-bytes. We realize you have lots of options to choose from when purchasing historical collectibles on eBay, so the fact you chose to do business with us is a great honor.

Please take a few moments to check your items over carefully when they arrive, and make sure they meet your expectations. Should you have any questions or concerns, please feel free to contact me personally. I will be happy to do whatever I can to make it right for you.

Could I also ask a small favor?

Here at history-bytes, we are always trying to make your shopping experience more enjoyable. Would you have a few moments to tell us about your experiences with history-bytes, and why you chose the particular items you did?

It will help us accomplish two important tasks:

1. *It will help us ensure a pleasant shopping experience for our customers.*
2. *It will help us to select more products that our customers want and need.*

To make it as easy as possible, just click reply to this email and tell us what you like or don't like about shopping with history-bytes. Next, tell us a little bit about why you purchased your item, and how you intend to use it. Finally, tell us what other items you would like to see us carry.

Thanks again for making your purchase from history-bytes. If you took the time to complete our survey—you're amazing. Rest assured, we will use that info to make your shopping experience with history-bytes even better.

Have a great day!

That's all there is to it. Take our survey. Make it your own. Feel free to change it up a bit and personalize it for your business. Ask about specific products, different parts of the shopping experience, or what customers liked or didn't like about your eBay store or listings.

You will be surprised what you learn. It just may help you rocket your sales to a new level.

....

If you are new to eBay and don't have any customers to survey, you're going to have to work things a little differently. Most of your research is going to focus on analyzing sales trends and using your gut instincts to determine how that data affects you.

The first thing you need to do is conduct an advanced search for items similar to what you plan to sell.

If you have never run an advanced search before—don't panic. It's super easy to do. Look for the search box at the top of the eBay page. Just to the right of it, you will see the word "advanced." Click on it.

This takes you to the advanced search page. I know, it seems overwhelming at first, but you will figure it out quickly.

The most important thing you need to understand is the only information that counts is what you find in sold listings. Anybody can list anything they want to on eBay and ask for a crazy amount of money. The way we separate the wheat from the chaff and get to the good stuff is by only analyzing completed sales where people spent money to buy something.

This tells us the seller did something right with their listing.

If you're with me so far.

Pick an item you are interested in selling and run an advanced search. Count how many items sold in the last thirty days (hint: they are listed in green). Now count how many didn't sell (hint: they are listed in red). Divide the number that sold by the total number of items that were listed. Doing this tells you the percentage of items that closed successfully. The most recent number I've seen is 42% of auction listings posted on eBay sell successfully.

Hopefully, the number you get will be somewhere between 40% and 50%.

Now it's time to dig deeper into the items that sold.

- Were they listed as an auction or fixed price?
- What was the high and low selling price?
- What was the average selling price?
- Did the auction listing use buy it now? If so, how many buyers used buy it now to purchase the item?
- Did the fixed price listing use best offer? If so, how many buyers used it to buy the item?
- What prices did sellers start their auction listings at?
- How many pictures did sellers use in their listings?
- What keywords did sellers use in their titles? What keywords did sellers use in their descriptions?
- How was the item description worded? Did the seller use bullet points? Lots of white space? Or, lots of description?
- Did the seller offer free shipping?
- Did the seller use flat rate or calculated shipping?
- What was the average shipping price?

These are just a few of the questions you want to ask yourself as you research your market. The more information you have, the easier it's going to be to pick items that sell and craft superior item descriptions.

The next thing you want to do is check out your competition.

If you followed through with the exercise listed above, you already discovered some sellers in your potential niche. Run another advanced search for an item you are considering selling.

Visit the seller's eBay store.

Check out the design first. Does the seller have a custom storefront? Do they have a custom listing header with categories and search features? Do they have store categories set up (usually there's a category list to the left of the store items)? Are they using promotional boxes to feature their items or shipping rates?

This is going to give you some good general information and help you to understand what you're up against. Take a look at how many feedbacks each seller has, and record the name of the top five sellers. You may even want to sign up for their store newsletters. This will help you do some strategic spying on your competitors.

When you are finished looking at the store, click into some of the categories and see what items sellers are offering. How broad is their product line? Do they sell at the low or high end of the price spectrum? And, finally—how many items are listed in their store?

It's a lot of information to digest, but by the time you are done, you are going to know a lot about your competition.

The next part of your plan is to put it all together. Examine what your top three to five competitors are doing. Look at their price, their shipping charges, their product line, and the way their items are listed.

Ask yourself –

1. What products aren't they offering that buyers in that niche would want?
2. What products, services, or features can you add to the mix that would make you stand out compared to these sellers?

3. Do you want to compete on price? Service? A broader product line?
4. What shipping strategy do you need to use—free? Low price? Etc.?
5. What tone do you need to set in your listings to attract buyers away from your competitors? Do you need to be serious, humorous, or just offer a more complete listing?

It's a lot of work, but if you do it all you are going to know your competition, and what it's going to take to attract buyers to your eBay listings.

Uncover Your Niche

The real key to success on eBay today is to cultivate a niche and carefully grow it by adding a steady stream of new products.

A lot of people get started selling on eBay by selling everything but the kitchen sink. They sell spare items they find around the house. Then they begin selling items they find at garage sales, yard sales, and estate sales. Sometimes it works, but it's a tough sell because it's hard to get repeat customers when you're selling a mish-mash of stuff.

To be successful, you need to build your tribe of fanatical customers who keep returning to your eBay store to see what's next? You need them to keep asking themselves, what crazy or unique item did this guy find now?

If you can develop even one hundred regular customers, who check back every week or every month for new items you're going to be extremely successful selling on eBay.

....

The definition of a niche is a subset or small portion of a larger market.

For example—clothing isn't a niche. Women's clothing isn't a niche. Plus sized women's work suits or plus sized women's swimwear is a niche.

Books aren't a niche. Books about Western Americana are a very general niche. Antiquarian books about Western bad men are a niche, as are vintage illustrated children's books.

Ideally, your niche should be in an area you enjoy and have at least some knowledge of. You're going to be spending a lot of time with it. The more you know about your niche, the products in it, and how to determine their condition the easier it's going to be to source and sell products.

....

When I first started selling on eBay, I was all over the board. I sold old clothes, unwanted household items, etc. After that, I started specializing in movies on DVD and VHS, and then vintage sports cards from the 1950's and 1960's.

I made a lot of sales, and I had some repeat buyers, but I wasn't making a lot of money. I bought the videos online from wholesalers in 100 and 500 case lots. Many of the movies would sell for $2.00 or $3.00 each. I paid $1.00 each, so I was making a few bucks. After a couple of months, I would package up the movies that didn't sell into lots of 25, 50, or 100 and start them at 50¢ each. That allowed me to break even on the dogs, or make a few cents on them.

I soon learned movies were a large market on eBay, but they were too competitive for me to make a decent profit.

Sports cards were another market I made a lot of sales in.

Early on, I determined to concentrate on the fifties and sixties baseball cards with a sprinkling of football cards. Over time, I developed a strong following of customers.

I wasn't doing anything special. I would buy "lots" and "partial" sets on eBay and Yahoo. I would break them up and resell the individual cards for one to ten dollars each. Every few months I would package up the cards that didn't sell into lots organized by team or year.

I made a lot of small dollar sales and developed a strong following of regular customers, but I never hit a home run. I couldn't make a living on what I was doing. It was more like a hobby that paid dividends.

I was stuck. I didn't have the money to move up to the big dollar cards, and I didn't want to remain a bottom feeder forever, so I cut the cord—disposed of my inventory and moved on.

....

It was about that time I discovered a guy selling magazine articles on eBay. It seemed crazy, but I followed his listings for a while, and he was making some decent sales. Nothing to write home to mom about, but…it appeared to me there was an opportunity to take it a few steps beyond what he was doing.

I poked around eBay to see if any other sellers were doing the same thing, and he pretty much had the market cornered at that time. There were several sellers offering vintage magazine advertisements and prints. One or two other sellers were hawking vintage car literature, advertising, and service manuals.

What I saw convinced me there was an opportunity here. I picked up an 1865 issue of *Harper's New Monthly Magazine* on eBay for fifteen bucks and jumped in. My fifteen bucks turned into $250, and over the next year, it grew to over $10,000 in sales.

Even though I didn't know it for quite some time, I had stumbled into a profitable niche. Several years later I was interviewing for a sales position at a car dealership. After some discussion about what I did on eBay, the sales manager came out and asked me how I got the idea.

"You stole it from someone else, didn't you?" I just nodded my head, waiting to see where he was going with this.

"It's ok," he continued, "the best ideas are the ones we borrow."

He was right. I stole the idea, but I refined it and developed it into a unique niche by specializing in history, biography, and science. Over time I added vintage prints, War of 1812 newspapers, and Spanish-American War prints.

My niche was a work in process. It was, and still is, constantly evolving based on customer needs, and new products I stumble across.

That's the story about how I got started in my eBay business. $411,000 in sales later it's starting to implode on me. The economy is some of the problem. My biggest buyers were universities, museums, libraries, researchers, and small publishers. A good deal of their funding dried up after 2008. Changes in the eBay platform took their toll, especially the move away from auction listings. The influx of fixed price listings made most of my items nearly impossible to discover in search.

A smart seller would have thrown in the towel years ago, but I kept rebuilding my broken brand, attempting to breathe new life into it.

It's still good for a few thousand dollars a month, but…the writing is on the wall. Next year I will be back selling in a newer more profitable niche.

....

Here are a few ideas to help you discover your niche.

1. **Take your time**. Many sellers stumble across the perfect niche like I did. Keep an eye on what's selling well on eBay, Amazon, and other e-commerce websites. Watch the news and TV entertainment programs. Follow blogs and read your local newspaper.

Even better, just watch the people around you. Grab a seat in the food court at the mall and listen to what people are talking about. Check out which stores they visit, and which ones they avoid.

The majority of people couldn't spot a new trend if it reached out and smacked them in the face. We don't notice them until they become part of our lives. That's why, so few of us made a killing with Microsoft, Apple, AOL, or any of the other high-tech companies. Trends nudge their way into our lives. At first, they are invisible, and over time they become commonplace.

A niche is a lot like a new trend. It's right there in front of you every day. It's just hard to see until you open your eyes, and let it in.

2. **Make sure your niche** has enough potential customers to keep you busy and make the income you are looking for. If a niche is too narrow or specialized, you are going to run out of people to sell to.

Here's an example of what I mean. When I first started selling on eBay, there was a guy selling back issues of several publications from the State Historical Society of Iowa. He was getting $15 to $30 an issue and was making ten to fifteen sales a week. Not too bad.

I did a little more digging and discovered the State Historical Society had a huge trove of issues and would sell you as many as you wanted for 50¢ or $1.00 a copy.

That's a nice profit margin, but the potential was limited. The market for Iowa history on eBay was too small. It offered a good part time income for this one seller, but it wouldn't work on a larger scale.

Unless. I contacted almost every historical society in the United States to inquire about the cost of back issues. What I discovered was it would be almost impossible to make a go of it. A few states like Missouri and Wyoming offered back issues at prices similar to Iowa. Most states wanted at least $5.00 per copy. Others, like California, recognized the value of what they had and priced them accordingly at $10.00, $20.00, or more per copy.

That confirmed it wasn't a profitable enough niche to build a real business on. Keep this in mind as you're searching for a niche because the sooner you find it's a bust—the more time and money you will save.

3. **You need to have a ready supply** of new product available to fuel your growth.

You can find the hottest niche out there, but if you can't get your hands on enough products to sell, you're not going to make it. If you are selling a vintage product, there needs to be enough of it available for you to have a ready supply. If you are selling a handmade craft or other product, ask yourself if you can supply enough products profitably to make it worthwhile. If you are purchasing a product to resell from a wholesaler look at all of your costs and ensure you can charge enough to recoup your costs and still make a respectable profit.

Don't just look at the cost. Consider how much shipping to you and your end user is going to be. Think about how much wiggle room you have on price. When you first start selling a new product, you might be the only one offering it, or there may be just a few of you, but as your niche grows—more and more sellers are going to jump in.

One problem I had was my inventory cost virtually nothing, but because of how many listings I ran to sell them—my eBay fees were out of this world. eBay fees could easily add $8.00 to $10.00 to an item that cost me 25 cents or less.

New sellers popped up every few months and soon faded away, because they didn't understand the real cost of making a sale. They assumed because the initial cost was cheap—they could undersell me, offering the same product for $5.00 or $10.00. The economic truth was they lasted three to six months and disappeared from eBay.

You need to have a ready supply of product available, and you need to be able to sell it at a profitable price otherwise you won't succeed.

4. **You'll hear many eBay sellers say** you need to corner the market on your niche to make it on eBay. I'm not so sure about that. If there's no competition for the products you want to sell it can only mean two things. Either it's a totally new product never before seen, or there's no market for it—other sellers have tried it and given up.

If you research your market and there's no one else out there selling the same product or niche on eBay, you need to ask yourself why.

It may be there is a limited supply of product available or a limited demand. It may be too new for enough people to know what it is. It may be too difficult to ship, or too expensive to ship.

Before you jump into a niche, investigate it thoroughly and completely understand it.

Sell a few products, and slowly test the waters.

5. **Make sure your niche is broad enough** to let you expand and add new products over time.

I started out selling magazine articles. As time when by, I slowly added prints, vintage newspapers, and other paper items. Several times I built niche stores offering rock n roll and sports memorabilia.

Make sure your niche is big enough to add new products and expand into new markets. Keep testing new items, and if they sell well, consider opening a new eBay store that caters to your niche.

It's not easy to find and build a niche, but it is the most profitable way to sell on eBay. When you've hit the right niche you won't have to look for customers; they'll come looking for you.

Ship Like a Pro

Understanding how to ship the items you sell is just as important as knowing which items to sell.

Online sellers face two types of shipping situations: domestic (shipping within your home country) and international (shipping outside of your home country). Many sellers spend years trying their hardest to avoid making international sales because they're afraid of the extra paperwork involved or that there may be excessive damage claims, theft, or negative feedback caused by shipping or communication glitches.

The truth is international shipping is no more difficult than domestic shipping. It's just a matter of learning and getting used to the extra paperwork involved.

Domestic Shipping

Most of the shipping you are going to do is considered domestic shipping, or shipping within your home country.

The Post Office offers many ways to ship items. The shipping method you choose depends on the item you are shipping, its size, value, and how quickly you want it to arrive.

Here is a breakdown of the most common shipping services available from the post office, and the different items you can ship with them.

- **Media mail** is designed to ship books, CDs, DVDs, and other educational materials. Media mail does have a few restrictions. The material cannot contain any advertising pages, so most magazines are ineligible for media mail shipping.

    Packages sent by media mail are subject to inspection by the Post Office, so if you do include ineligible items, they can send the items back to you postage due. The main advantage to sellers from using media mail is it's cheaper to ship heavier items like books. As a result, you can offer your customers a less expensive delivery option. This is especially important if you are selling in the book category because eBay requires sellers to offer an option priced at $4.00 or less.

    Delivery time is normally 3 to 8 business days but can vary based on the season. At Christmas time it can take as long as two to three weeks to deliver a media mail package so be sure to give buyers a heads up – "Hey. It's cheap, but it's slow." That way they understand it's the post office, not you.

- **First Class**. If you're shipping smaller items (less than 13 oz.) first class is going to be the most economical method available. You can ship just about anything—books, clothes, DVDs, CD's, jewelry, stamps, postcards, you name it.

Tracking is not available on all first class packages, so you cannot offer proof of delivery.

If you are mailing flat items like baseball cards and postcards, then you cannot add tracking. Your package is required to be a minimum of 1/8" thick. Delivery time is normally 1 to 3 days depending on where you are sending your package.

- **Priority Mail**. The majority of items sold by online sellers ship by priority mail. It has several advantages over other services including:
1) You can mail heavier items than first class,
2) Most items deliver within 1 to 3 days, and
3) Tracking is available for all packages, so you have proof of delivery for eBay and your customers, and
4) The Post Office provides free shipping materials, so you don't have to invest in boxes and other expensive packaging materials.
5) You can schedule a pickup, and the post office will send a carrier to your home or business to pick up your packages.

The disadvantage to using priority mail is that it is more expensive than first class or media mail.

- **Priority Mail Flat Rate** takes the guess work out of shipping. You can ship whatever will fit in the package regardless of the weight anywhere in the United States for a preset fee. This is a great option for buyers and sellers because it's less expensive to ship heavier items or multiple items that will fit into a single package.

Like regular priority mail—it's quick, offering 1 to 3-day delivery, comes with delivery confirmation, and packaging materials are free from the Post Office. Be sure you use the Flat Rate Priority Mail boxes when using this service.

- **Standard Post** is a less expensive option for mailing parcels and oversize packages. The normal delivery time is 2 to 8 business days. Tracking is included in your shipping fees.

- **Express Mail** offers overnight delivery service to most areas in the United States. If your customer needs an item quick, this is the service for them. Be aware it's expensive, and the fees depend on the size and weight of the package you are sending.

  Like Priority Mail, Express Mail offers free packaging materials and delivery confirmation. Sellers also receive $100 of insurance free with most parcels sent, and signature delivery confirmation which eBay and PayPal require on more expensive packages.

- **Priority Mail Express Flat Rate** offers next day delivery (in most areas), plus the added convenience of simplified rates. When you use the flat rate boxes anything you mail in them (regardless of weight) ships for one fee, so if you're shipping heavy items—this is the service for you.

To get the full scoop on these delivery services, check out the following link. https://www.usps.com/ship/compare-domestic-services.htm

Package Your Items Like a Pro

How you package the items you sell makes a major difference in how buyers view you as a seller.

If you just toss your items into a box or envelope, it's going to leave a sour taste in the minds of your buyers. Their purchases are likely to arrive damaged or with bumped and scuffed up packaging that looks like it's been run through the ringer.

I know many books recommend recycling used boxes, packing materials, and such to use for your shipping. In my mind—that's the worst mistake you can make.

You only get one chance to make a good first impression. If your package arrives all scuffed up, or with all sorts of squiggly lines where you crossed out previous addresses, customers are going to be concerned about their purchases. If that's the way you package stuff, your buyers are going to think "God help me" about the stuff you put inside the box.

Set Up Your Shipping Station

Most sellers I've worked with ship their items from the same desk they sell from. If you're a part-time seller, that's okay. If you eBay for a living, I'd recommend a separate shipping station.

Here's why.

Shipping is a specialized task. To do it right you need a lot of space and all of your packaging materials and supplies nearby. I have a separate desk and table set up for shipping. I only use my shipping computer when I'm shipping items or tracking shipments. It's an older castoff, but it serves the purpose. I have two printers hooked up to it...a Zebra LP 2844 and a Samsung laser printer.

Most of my shipping labels get printed on the Zebra. I use the laser printer to print packing slips and thank you cards. I also have a postal scale that attaches to the computer through the USB port. It's digital and can accurately weigh up to twenty-five pounds in one-ounce increments. The weight automatically gets transferred into Stamps.com with one click of my mouse, so there's never any guesswork involved. I normally round up to the next ounce to add a little wiggle room for tape or the label.

I have sturdy warehouse shelving set up opposite to my desk. The bottom row has flat boxes in various sizes. The next shelf has priority mail boxes and envelopes. The shelf above that has stay flat mailers and padded mailers. The top shelf has all of my miscellaneous supplies—shipping labels, paper, extra rolls of tape, box cutters, and Sharpie markers.

Everything is nearby. Once I get started, I can normally package and ship thirty or forty items in an hour. Before I had my shipping station, it always took twice as long because I was running from here to there looking for stuff, or trying to find a good spot to spread all my stuff out.

Must Have Supplies

There is certain equipment and supplies you need to keep on hand so you can ship smart.

>> **Packaging material**. Make sure to stock up on boxes, padded mailers, stay flat mailers, bubble wrap, and tape. The worst thing that can happen is to be in the middle of packaging up your orders, and then discover you don't have the supplies you need.

If you ship priority or express mail stop by the post office and pick up the supplies you need. Better yet, hop online and check out https://store.usps.com/store/browse/category.jsp?categoryId=shipping-supplies. Order your boxes ten, twenty-five, or more at a time depending upon how quick you go through them. The post office will deliver them free within two to three days.

If you need to purchase boxes, padded mailers, or stay flat mailers—consider Uline - http://www.uline.com/. They have decent prices and quick delivery.

Wal-Mart carries a great selection of boxes in their shipping supply aisle. The prices are good, especially when you compare them to the big box office supply stores.

I've also had good luck buying supplies from several suppliers on eBay.

Value Mailers
http://stores.ebay.com/VALUEMAILERS?_trksid=p2047675.l2563

. Royal Mailers
http://stores.ebay.com/Royalmailers?_trksid=p2047675.l2563

>> **Postal scale**. If you sell online, you need a postal scale. I know a lot of sellers try to fudge it and just guess at weights. Trust me. No one is that good. Every ounce you guess wrong costs you at least seventeen cents. Over the course of a year that's going to cost you one hundred dollars or more.

Best advice: buy a good digital scale. You can find scales with weight capacities starting at five pounds. I recommend choosing a scale from USPS.com. They have a good selection, and they hold up well.

>> **Printer**. The printer you use is a matter of preference. I like to use a Zebra label printer because it prints a small compact label you can peel off and stick on your package. There's no messing with tape, or ink cartridges because it's a thermal printer. The next best choice is a laser printer. The ink is less expensive, and it prints quicker. There's nothing more aggravating than waiting for a slow ink jet printer to finish printing your label. The last choice is an ink jet printer. It's slow, but it will get the job done. If you use adhesive-backed labels an ink jet printer is your best bet. Whenever I tried them in my laser printer, they were too thick and jammed it up.

>> **Shipping tape**. I usually pick up my tape at SAMs Club or Walmart. You can buy single rolls or save a few bucks and buy them in six packs. My only recommendation is not to buy the cheapest tape you can find. It tears, it splits, and it's a mess restarting the roll.

>> **Bubble wrap**. If you are packaging china, old books, or other fragile items you're going to need bubble wrap. Here's one item it's okay to reuse. Good places to purchase bubble wrap are SAMs Club, Walmart, or online.

>> **Box cutter**. Be sure to keep a couple of box cutters and plenty of extra razor blades on hand. You want to package your items right, and the best way to do that is to give everything a snug tight fit. To do that you need a box cutter with a sharp blade so you can easily refit boxes.

>> **Peanuts** are those little white foam half circles shippers use to line their packages. They are all static filled and stick to everything. I hate them and refuse to buy anything else from sellers that use them. Use peanuts at your risk; they are a sticky mess.

Packaging Tips

Okay. You set up your shipping station and stocked up on supplies. Now it's time for *Packaging 101*.

The best tip I can give you is always to choose the right type of packaging, and err on the side of more packing materials, not less. Don't skimp on packing materials. It will come back to haunt you.

Tip #1. Choose the right type of packaging. If you are shipping a newer book or a paperback, it's okay to use a padded mailer. If you are shipping a rare book or vintage book, you need to package it differently. Use a box and make sure to place it inside a sealed plastic bag, and then wrapped with newspaper or bubble wrap. Doing this keeps the corners from getting scuffed or bent, and it protects the book from moisture damage should your box be exposed to water.

If you are shipping china, glass figurines or other fragile materials pick a box about six inches larger all around than what you are shipping. Line the box with bubble wrap or wadded up newspapers. Next, wrap each item in bubble wrap or newspaper and tape it up, so it is secure. Lay the item in the box and cover it with bubble wrap or newspaper. Continue doing this until the box is full. Build another layer of bubble wrap or wadded up newspapers at the top. You will know you've got it right when you shake the box. If something shifts or rattles inside, add more packing material.

When you ship electronics, laptops, or tablets, your best bet is to ship them in the original box. If that isn't possible, find a box just slightly larger than the item you're going to ship. Build a nest in the box using foam, bubble wrap, or wadded up newspapers. Place your item in a sealed plastic bag, to prevent moisture damage. Wrap it several times with bubble wrap. Place the item in the box. Wrap any accessories, discs, power cord, etc. separately and place them in the box. Build a nest around the top of the box before you seal it to ensure the item won't get damaged in transit. Tape all of the way around the circumference of the box, length wise and width wise. Doing this ensures the tape won't break free where the box can come open in shipment.

If you are shipping clothes, you can pop a shirt or t-shirt into a priority mail bag. If you are shipping jackets, jeans or multiple items use a flat rate priority mail box to reduce your costs. If you are unsure which is cheaper—regular priority mail or flat rate, weigh it out and let the numbers do the talking.

I'm not going to describe any more scenarios, just understand that you need to adapt every packing situation to the item you are shipping.

I have received close to a thousand packages over the last fifteen years. Some of them were perfectly packed, some were adequate, and quite a few arrived banged up and had the items I purchased hanging half way out of the box or missing.

Tip #2. The best time to decide how to pack an item for shipment is before you list it.

Think about it. If you list a computer or rare figurine—how are you going to determine shipping charges if you don't know how you're going to pack and ship it?

In my case, I have hundreds of rare newspapers dating from 1806 to the Civil War period, but I don't have a cost effective way to ship an individual paper to buyers. If I fold the paper to make the size manageable, I will ruin a good part of the items collectability. To ship a single paper would require me to buy an oversized casing for it, and then a custom box to put it in. Packaging could easily run forty to fifty dollars before shipping costs. That's a hefty chunk of change to add to a paper I'm selling for twenty-five dollars.

The economics don't work out in this case, so the papers remain in my private collection for now.

Make sure you are not going to go underwater on the items you sell. Before you list an item, determine what it's going to take to ship it. What kind of packaging materials do you need? How much is shipping likely to cost? Is the item expensive enough to require insurance? If so, how much is that going to cost?

Know what you are looking at up front because after the sale you can't come back and ask the customer for more money.

A lot of sellers box their items up at the time they list them. They weigh the package, input the weight into the eBay, shipping calculator. When the item sells, they grab the box, print a label and drop it in the mail.

I say to do whatever works for you.

Just keep in mind, buyers always have questions. You may need to open the box up to answer a question or to shoot a quick picture or two. Also, not every item sells. You may need to bundle that item up with several other items to make a sale.

Do I Need to Offer Free Shipping?

Free shipping is the biggest bugaboo confronting online sellers right now.

eBay encourages sellers to offer free shipping, and they promote items with free shipping to buyers. Because of this many new sellers think they must offer free shipping. Let me assure you: that's not true.

You don't have to offer free shipping on any of the items you sell. However, you may want to offer free shipping. Here's why?

Normally sales increase when you offer free shipping. There's something about "free" and "shipping" that makes buyers loosen up their purse strings and spend more money. I'm not sure what it is, but the word "free" is one of those magical keys that can get consumers to pull the trigger and spend more money.

Keep that info tucked away in the back of your head for a moment.

Just because eBay likes free shipping and consumers like free shipping doesn't mean it's the magical ingredient you have been searching for to increase your sales and profits. It needs to be the right combination that's good for both of you. That means you need to be able to make a profit, and your customer needs to get a good value when you offer free shipping.

How does that work?

If you are selling lightweight, easy to ship items free shipping should be a no brainer. Let me repeat that. If you're selling light items, you can ship in an envelope or padded mailer and ship for under a dollar you are probably better off giving your customer free shipping rather than trying to charge them that buck. So if you are selling postcards, baseball cards, small knickknacks, and inexpensive jewelry items that you mail in a regular envelope—mark your item up a buck, and give your customer free shipping.

If you are selling heavier items, low margin items, or custom made items free shipping may make sense. Before you pull the trigger, though, do your research. Investigate what other sellers with similar items are doing. If everyone else is offering free shipping, you are going to be better off following the pack, unless...and, this is a big unless. If everyone else has marked their item up enough to cover shipping, plus a couple of extra bucks for profit it might make sense to charge shipping and price your item as low as you can while still holding a decent profit.

If some sellers in your category offer free shipping, and some charge for shipping, you may want to test the waters. Offer a few items with free shipping, and a few with your regular shipping charges. Run with the method that makes the most sales for you.

If you are the only one selling a certain product and you are making a killer profit, go ahead and give your customers free shipping. It's like extra icing on the cake. It's one more reason to buy from you.

Katen Raj wrote one of the better discussions I have found on the web about free shipping on *CPC Strategy Blog*. Give it a look if you need a little extra help working through this issue. http://www.cpcstrategy.com/blog/2012/04/the-free-shipping-formula-for-online-retailers/

Nick Vulich

Setting Shipping Rates in eBay

Setting shipping rates is another tricky area that can confuse sellers.

Here's the least you need to know.

- If you're a Top-Rated Seller or want to be a Top-Rated Seller you are required to provide tracking information for all of your domestic sales. You are also required to post tracking information back into the listing on a minimum of 90% of the items you sell.
- Top-Rated Sellers are required to ship all of their items with a one day handling period.
- If the value of any item you sell is over $200, you are required to provide signature delivery confirmation.

If you're not a Top-Rated Seller and don't have any intention of becoming one, it's still a good idea to provide delivery confirmation on every item you send. It protects you from bad buyers who may open an item not received case because they know they will win if you can't provide proof of delivery.

Now, we will get down to the nitty-gritty of setting up shipping in your item listings.

To set your domestic shipping options look for the section labeled *add shipping details* on your sell your item form.

The first choice you need to make is to select your shipping method from the drop-down box. There are four possible choices: flat cost, calculated, freight, and no shipping—local pickup. Flat cost is where you charge all buyers the same shipping rate. Calculated shipping uses the eBay shipping calculator to figure shipping based upon your item weight and its destination. Freight is for larger items too big to ship by the USPS or UPS. Items shipping by freight are carried by a semi or common carrier.

If you sell large items that need to ship by common carrier keep in mind eBay's freight calculator only works up to 150 pounds. If your item exceeds 150 pounds, you need to use flat rate shipping. You also need to understand how truck lines work. Most carriers only require their drivers to pull your item to the back of the truck. It's up to your customer to have people available to help them get their item out of the truck and carry it inside the house.

You need to explain this to your customers in your listing description, and again in the shipping instructions you send the buyer after the sale. Here's another tip. You can request the truck line to call your customer the day before delivery. Sometimes they will do it; sometimes they don't, so try not to make too many promises.

To set up calculated shipping, click the blue lettering that says *calculate shipping*. A pop-up box will open up. Fill in the options, and you're good to go.

If you are using flat rate shipping, click in the box that says standard shipping. Select the shipping service you want to set up, and enter the shipping fee in the smaller box to the right where it says cost. If you want to offer free shipping for that service, put a check mark where it says free shipping. To offer more shipping options click the blue lettering that says *offer additional service*.

To offer local pickup, check the box where it says *Local Pickup*. Be careful when you select this option because local pickup is not available in all categories.

Think long and hard before you offer local pickup for your items. Do you really want to invite customers into your home? Over the years, I've had some local buyers insist on picking up their items to save on shipping. Most times I've delivered the items to their business or met the customer outside of McDonald's or another local business. It's less risky, but a major pain in the backside.

Best advice: avoid local pickup whenever possible.

If you set up flat shipping rules, you can check the box to apply them. If you would like to set up or edit your rules, click on the blue lettering that says *edit rules*. The pop-up box will walk you through setting up shipping discounts. If you edit the top set of rules, the changes are only good for the listing you are currently working on. If you want to create a discount for all of your listings you need to scroll down to the bottom of the pop-up box where it says Promotional Shipping Rule (applies to all items).

If you haven't used this feature before, you should give it a whirl. You would be surprised how many buyers will shop for additional items to save a few bucks on shipping.

The next choice you have is to select the *handling time*. If you are a Top-Rated Seller, you are required to ship all items within one day so be sure to select that option.

The final item gives you a nudge to add next day shipping to your listing. I don't offer the service unless buyers contact me and say they have to have next day shipping. My reason for not offering next day shipping is very few people request it, and you have deadlines you need to meet to get the item to the post office on time. It takes more effort than it's worth.

That's it. Your shipping options are done.

Here's another quick tip, so you don't have to go through this with every item you list—set up one of your listings as a template, or when you list new items pull up one of your old listings and select the option to sell a similar item. When you use either of these options, your previous info transfers over to the new listings. Use the info you want to keep, type over or delete the unwanted info.

Printing Shipping Labels Using eBay & PayPal

Both eBay and PayPal let sellers print shipping labels directly from their sites. The process is easy to use and lets you print professional looking labels and invoices to include with your shipments.

Print eBay Shipping Labels

The easiest way to print shipping labels using eBay is to go into your *Selling Manager*. In the left-hand column, find where it says *Selling Manager Pro*. Just down from there you will see the word *sold*. Select it.

That's going to bring up a list of your sold items. Locate the item you want to ship, and scroll over to the far right column labeled actions. The first thing you should see is *Print Shipping*.

When you select *Print Shipping,* it takes you to the eBay ship your item page. When you click on it, the page prepopulates with all of your item information.

At the top of the page, it shows the item description, the price paid shipping fee, shipping service paid for, and the expected delivery date. The left-hand column contains the shipping information—the buyer's address and your address. If you need to change the address, select where it says change, and enter the correct shipping information.

Just below the address details, you will see a box labeled Add message to buyer email. I have a standard thank you message in here, but you can use it to tell your buyer a little more about the item or direct them to your store specials. It's up to you.

The center column contains the package details. It's where you choose the carrier, add shipping options, and choose your mailing date. eBay has two approved carriers the United States Postal Service (USPS), and FedEx. My shipping experience has all been with the USPS, so that's what I'm going to cover here. If you ship using FedEx, select them as the carrier and follow the prompts to complete your shipment.

The first thing you need to do is select your carrier. In this case, choose USPS.

Use the next box to select your shipping service. The choices are priority mail, first class package, parcel select, media mail, and priority mail express. The priority mail and priority mail express options let you choose the level of service you want.

After you've selected your service, you have the option of printing the auction number or some other message on the label. Check the box and type in your message. The default message is the auction id.

You select the mailing date in the final box. The choices are today, tomorrow, or the next day. The reason for this is you are supposed to mail your package the same day you print the label, so if you are printing the label today, but not mailing your package for two days, you should change the date. I have never had a problem with the post office if I'm a day or two late dropping the package in the mail, but your local post office may see things differently.

The third column shows your postage cost broken down by the postage cost, the delivery confirmation fee, and the total cost. Below that, you have an option to hide the shipping so buyers can't see how much actual shipping costs you. It's your choice—if you are playing by the rules and charging actual shipping, let your buyers see the shipping cost. It will prove you're on the up-and-up.

Click purchase postage, and your PayPal account gets charged the shipping fees. The next screen will show a mockup of the label. You can print a sample, or print the label.

After the label prints, the program will automatically transfer tracking information into the item listing so buyers can follow the movement of their package.

Alternatively, you can print your postage labels directly from PayPal. To get started, open your PayPal account and locate the transaction you want to print the postage for. Click on the text where it says *Print shipping label*. It brings up the same shipping page we used above, so you can follow through using those directions.

Nick Vulich

Do I Need Insurance?

When eBay allowed sellers to charge customers for insurance, I required all my buyers to purchase it. It saved a lot of hassles. If the item got lost, the customer received a refund.

What I discovered after shipping over 30,000 items is very few items get lost, stolen, or damaged in transit. I think I have had two damaged packages, and three lost packages in fifteen years. So, is insurance necessary? It depends on you, and your tolerance for loss. Most of the items I ship cost between twenty to twenty-five dollars. Insurance costs close to two bucks for each package. Take two bucks times thirty thousand packages, and that's close to sixty thousand dollars.

My losses in all this time have amounted to under one hundred bucks. If I'd bought insurance on every item, I shipped I'd be out close to $60,000. When you look at it that way—insurance doesn't make sense.

But...insuring my more expensive packages does make me feel all warm and fuzzy inside. Because of that, I picked a number where I would insure my shipments. If the value exceeds that number I purchase insurance. For me, the magic number is fifty dollars. For you, it may be ten dollars or one hundred dollars. The best I can tell you is to choose your threshold for loss and make a decision to insure all shipments that exceed that number—that way you can sleep nights.

Here's the least you need to know about insurance.

- eBay no longer allows sellers to charge buyers for insurance. You can roll it into your shipping costs, or you can bury it in the cost of your item.
- Filing an insurance claim with the Post Office is a pain in the rear end. It takes a minimum of thirty days for the post office to reimburse you. Many times it can take two or three times that long.
- When you sell something on eBay, it's hard to prove the actual value of an item, especially for collectibles and one-of-a-kind items. Just because you paid five bazillion dollars for a rare candy bar wrapper doesn't mean that's the value of your item.
- You may have insurance, but your customer doesn't care about that. They don't want to wait thirty days or more to get their money back. If you make them wait for a refund odds are you're going to receive negative feedback.

With all of that said, how do you file an insurance claim? The easiest way is to do it online. Go to the following link https://www.usps.com/ship/file-domestic-claims.htm. It will walk you through filing an insurance claim for a lost parcel.

Here are a few of the highlights to keep in mind.

You need to upload tracking info for the item, a copy of the sales receipt or your eBay auction listing number (to prove value), your insurance receipt, and if you received a damaged item—you need to save the item, along with all packaging materials until the claim finishes processing.

If for some reason you can't file the online claim call (800) 275-8777, and they will send you a claim form.

Using a Third-Party Shipping Provider

eBay's shipping label service is great, but sometimes you need a little more oomph to boost your sales and simplify things even more.

I've been using Stamps.com for nearly ten years, and it's been a great alternative for me. Other people have had good luck using Endicia to handle their shipping needs. Both services charge a monthly service fee for using them.

I know what you're thinking. Wait a minute Nick; I'm trying to save money, not spend even more.

Believe me, I understand. The thing is I save a lot of money using Stamps.com to power my eBay shipping. Here's why I use it, and how it saves me money.

What got me hooked on Stamps.com is it's the only way I can ship my items first class international without going to the post office and having them print labels for me. If you use eBay's shipping solution or Click-N-Ship,® you can only ship internationally using priority or express mail. When I do that, international sales go down because of the extra shipping costs involved. The extra sales I get by offering the less expensive shipping solution more than cover the $15.99 monthly fee.

One of the other reason I like using Stamps.com is it collects information from all of the platforms I sell on and lets me handle all of my shipping from one central location. For me, that means I can ship the items I sell on eBay, Amazon, bid Start, and my website all from the same program console.

I don't have to jump from site to site to ship everything. If I need to look up shipping info for an item—it's all in Stamps.com.

It's convenient. I like that. It's worth the extra fifteen dollars a month it costs me to use the service.

To get started with Stamps.com click on the following link http://www.stamps.com/. Select get started to register for a new account. Most times they offer a sign up special that gives you a free postal scale, $25.00 in free shipping credits, and miscellaneous other goodies, along with a one-month free trial.

Once you are good to go, you can connect all of your seller accounts.

What I'm going to do next is give you a quick walkthrough on how to connect your seller accounts, and how to print postage using Stamps.com. (I assume Endicia works similar to this but I've never used that service so I can't provide you with specifics.)

Don't worry. I'll make this quick and painless.

Setup Shipping Accounts

There are two ways to set up your accounts. Select *Manage Sources* in the toolbar at the top of the screen, or select *batch* from the toolbar in the left-hand column.

Choose Create Profile, and select the data source you want to create.

Printing Postage

When you open your Stamp.com dashboard, there is a command bar running across the top of the screen. There are four main tabs that you'll use over and over again: import orders, manage sources, print, and add order.

- Import orders lets you collect your orders from all of the sites you sell on and bring them into Stamps.com.
- Manages sources lets you add, delete, or edit data streams.
- Add order allows you to print a label for a package where the customer is not included in any of your data streams. An example is when I send out a review copy of one of my books. The recipient is not in my data stream, so I need to set up a one-time shipment.
- Print pulls up the screen to print your shipping label.

Okay, let's assume you just sat down at your desk and you are ready to start shipping. What do you do?

Select <import orders> from the top menu bar; you'll be prompted several times about actions that are in progress. Most often Stamps.com wants permission to update addresses to match the official address in the postal system computer. Click okay.

After a little while, all your orders will appear in a spreadsheet in the middle of the screen. Select the item you want to mail, and click on the recipient name. This will open up the shipping screen for that customer.

Off to the left-hand side of the screen, it displays your name and address. Below that, you will see the customer's name and address. You can make whatever changes you need to the shipping address here. The next line is labeled email address. Check the box in front of it, and it will populate with your customer's email address. When you check this, it will send shipping and tracking info to your buyer. The box right after this is cost code. You can make an internal note here if you are tracking categories for shipping.

The next column contains your shipping options.

If you have a USB scale, it will transfer the weight with the click of a button. I usually round up to the next ounce or two depending on the item I'm shipping. That gives me a little wiggle room for the label and tape.

After this, you need to choose the type of mail piece—package, thick envelope, etc.

Then you select the mail class —

- First Class
- Priority Mail
- Express Mail
- Parcel Post
- Media Mail

Place a check mark on the tab to select the mail class. When you do this, it will show the cost for that service. Some classes display as blanked out if you can't choose them to ship that particular item. As an example, packages over thirteen ounces cannot ship by first class so that shipping method would not be available for you to select.

After this, you choose tracking options—delivery confirmation (free with most shipping methods), signature confirmation (an additional $2.35), or none (tracking is not available on flats sent by first class).

Just below this, there is a line labeled options where you can add—certified, USPS insurance, registered, or COD delivery.

The next option lets you select insurance. You can select none or Stamps.com. Your final choice is whether you want to hide the postage cost so buyers cannot see it. If you mark your shipping up, be sure to choose this option.

After you select all your options, click <save> at the bottom of the box. A green circle should appear in front of the <order id> on the spreadsheet. To print your postage, choose <print> from the menu bar at the top of the screen. You should see a pop-up that shows the printer name and details. Select <print> at the bottom of the screen to print your label.

International Shipping with Stamps.com

Setting up an order for international delivery is very similar to shipping a domestic order. The only difference is you need to complete a customs form.

Here what you need to do to fill out the online customs form.

Click on the customs form, and it will display a pop-up box for you to fill out. At the top of the form, it asks for a phone number. If your customer provided a number to eBay, it would prepopulate. If they did not give a phone number, I just fill in 999-999-9999. Otherwise, it will not let you continue.

Where it asks for contents, you have several options. Choose <merchandise>. In the box next to this type a short description. I usually type article or print.

About midway down the page, there is a section labeled *itemized package contents*. The first box asks for the quantity or number of items in your package. After that, you need to provide a short description of the item. It should prepopulate from your eBay item description. If the description is too long, you need to shorten it, or the form will not process properly. The next item it asks you for is the weight of just the item (without the packaging).

When you've completed all of the items, the box at the end of this line asks you to *add item*. Check that box, and it will move your description into the box below that line.

At the bottom of the pop-up box is a form you need to check. It begins with "I acknowledge…" Once you select the check box, the pop-up box disappears, and you can print your item like normal.

Sell International

Here's a secret many online sellers don't know. The fastest growing sellers on eBay are powering that growth with international sales. According to a recent article on Linnworks, "76% of [the] fastest growers are primarily trading across borders."

The beauty of selling internationally is when the domestic economy slows down and sales in your country become sluggish, there are still pockets of growth and increasing demand in foreign economies. The key to tapping into these growth pockets is to make your items available to sellers in those countries.

I started listing items internationally in 2001, and within a year thirty to thirty-five percent of my orders were shipping overseas. Over the last fourteen years, I completed nearly 5,000 international transactions with only two lost packages.

If you are on the line about getting started with international shipping—consider baby-stepping it. Start with proven foreign trade partners like Canada, the United Kingdom, and Australia. There are few language barriers dealing with these countries. You should also consider selling to Germany. According to a recent article in *Forbes Magazine*, Germany and the United Kingdom account for 48 percent of all international sales made on eBay.

To qualify for international visibility on eBay sellers must meet several standards.

- Have a verified PayPal account tied to their eBay seller account
- PayPal needs to be offered as a payment option
- Must have 10 or more positive feedbacks
- Items must be listed in the appropriate category
- Need to enable shipping to countries you want to ship in
- For best visibility sellers must specify the levels of shipping service, they are offering

The other great thing is if you sell using your eBay.com account your feedback will be visible to sellers on eBay's foreign sites.

If you are a seller in the United States and specify you will ship to Canada, your items will automatically display on eBay.ca.

Items listed on international sites do not count as duplicate listings, so sellers don't get penalized for listing the same item on different eBay sites.

eBay gives you four ways to make your items available to international buyers.

1. Opt into eBay's Global Shipping Program.
2. Enable your items for international shipping.
3. List your items on international sites.
4. Open eBay stores in countries where you do a large amount of business.

What I'm going to do next is look at each option in more detail and explain who it is for, and how you can get started using it.

eBay Global Shipping Program

Several years ago, eBay introduced their Global Shipping Program. It's an easy way for sellers to jump into international selling without having to worry about shipping rules, customs forms, etc.

If you have been itching to get started with international sales, but were afraid of the extra work involved I suggest giving it a shot using eBay's Global Shipping Program.

Many small sellers are terrified of international shipping. They have heard so many horror stories; they are scared to give it a shot. They don't want to fill out customs forms or worry about whether their package is going to make it all the way to Timbuktu or not.

eBay has eliminated all of that grief for sellers who use their Global Shipping Program. Sellers list their items just like they normally would. When the item sells they ship it to an eBay shipping center in the United States.

Bing Badda Boom! As soon as it arrives at the shipping center, your responsibility for the shipment is over. From that point on eBay and their shipping partners assume all responsibility for getting your package to its destination.

Here's how it works.

When you list your item for sale on eBay check the box to include your item in the Global Shipping Program, and you're good to go.

Some categories don't qualify for inclusion in the Global Shipping Program. When you bump into these eBay will flag the item and let you know. I do a lot of selling in the collectibles category. Collectibles manufactured before 1899 don't qualify, so I see this issue pop up quite often. The only way around it is to ship the item internationally yourself. I'll discuss this option in more detail later.

When an item sells using the Global Shipping Program sellers can't send the buyer an invoice. eBay takes care of all this for you. The reason is you have no way to know what their shipping fee will be.

Once the customer pays, you will receive your payment notice along with the shipping address. An easy way to recognize a payment made through the Global Shipping Program is the address will include a long reference number.

Ship your item like you normally would. Include delivery confirmation so you can be sure the item gets received at the shipping center. Once you have confirmation the item was received, your part in the transaction is complete.

eBay's shipping partner—Pitney Bowes—will readdress the item, fill out all of the appropriate customs forms, and ensure your item delivers to the customer.

That's the way it should happen. Now and then things don't work out as planned—the customer doesn't receive the item, or it arrives damaged. As a seller, you're supposed to be protected from receiving negative feedback in such a situation. That's true to a point. You need to keep an eye on your feedback profile and keep after eBay to update it when errors are made.

I received a negative feedback due to a customer not receiving their item. I knew it wasn't received because that's what the seller wrote in his feedback. So I called eBay customer service and explained the problem. After about fifteen minutes of researching the problem, the rep agreed I was not responsible. He removed the negative feedback while we were still on the phone.

If you experience a similar problem, contact eBay customer service immediately. When you call, have the listing item number and the feedback information available and ready to share with them. Make it easy for eBay to help you.

Overall, the Global Shipping Program is a great way to increase your sales. At my peak selling period, international sales accounted for roughly thirty-five to forty percent of my eBay sales and profits.

If you are looking for an effortless method to grow your sales opt into the Global Shipping Program and give it a shot.

Enable Items for International Shipping

We have already talked about eBay's Global Shipping Program and how easy it is to use, so why would anybody want to ship international packages on their own?

That's a great question.

It comes down to having more control over your shipping options, and the ability to make more sales. When you use eBay's Global Shipping Program, they figure in custom's fees, a markup to pay themselves and their shipping partner an additional profit, plus actual shipping costs. The final number eBay shows your customer for shipping can be mind-boggling and can cost you the sale.

Let me use the products I sell as an example. When I ship items internationally on my own, I charge $5.00 to ship items to Canada, and $9.00 for shipping anywhere else in the world. Sometimes I make a few extra bucks, sometimes I lose a few bucks, but over time it averages out. Keep in mind; the buyer is still on the line for duty and customs fees when their item arrives.

When I sell the same item using eBay's Global Shipping Program they charge my customer in the low twenty dollar range for Canada, and in the low thirty dollar range for Europe and the rest of the world. My items normally sell for sixteen to twenty-five dollars, so customers are confronted with some serious sticker shock when they see eBay's shipping price.

Self-preservation is one of the major reasons I ship most international packages myself.

What I'm going to do now is walk you through setting up the international portion of your eBay sell your item form. It's structured very similar to how you set up your domestic shipping options so it should be easy to follow along and use.

....

Everything you need to set your international shipping options is located in the box labeled *International Shipping*.

Your first choice is to opt into the Global Shipping Program. In this case, you want to leave that box unchecked.

Below this, you have a drop-down box that offers you the option to select flat rate, calculated shipping, or no additional options. As a quick review flat rate shipping is where you have one set shipping fee for all buyers, calculated shipping uses the eBay shipping calculator to determine the shipping price based on the shipping destination. The difference is—flat rate shipping is easier to set up and use, but calculated shipping can give buyers closer to you a break in shipping costs thus giving you the opportunity to grab additional sales from price conscious buyers.

After you choose your shipping method, you'll see another drop down box that says shipping. It gives you three choices: worldwide, chose a custom location, or Canada. I normally set up a separate price for worldwide and Canada—any more is overkill in my book. However, if you ship a lot of packages to Mexico, the UK or wherever go ahead and set up a special price for them too. The drop down box next to this lets you choose the type of service you wish to offer, and the box to the right of that lets you set your shipping price.

Below this, you see a line labeled *offer additional service*. You can use this to ship to an additional location or to offer a different delivery method.

In the *additional ship to locations*, you can check off the areas you are willing to ship to, and the buyer can contact you for more details. Some sellers have lots of rules about where they will and will not ship too. A lot of sellers mark Malaysia, Italy, Mexico, Russia, etc. off limits because it's all over the internet that other people have experienced problems when they ship packages there. In my book that's all talk. I've shipped items to all those countries and never had a problem. All I'm saying is if you're going to put areas off limits or discourage buyers from certain regions wait until you have a problem with the area, then evaluate the situation and determine how you want to handle it.

The final line—combined shipping discounts, lets you apply your discount rules to this purchase if you set them up. My items are light and only add a few ounces to the package. Therefore, I ship all additional items for free. It's a great way to encourage buyers to continue shopping with you. If you can't offer to ship all additional items for free—consider offering discounted shipping for additional purchases. It will bring you more business over the long haul.

That's it. You're open for international business. Sit back and wait for the orders to roll in.

I'm going to make one additional suggestion here. Take a few moments to help set buyer expectations. International buyers are similar to domestic buyers—they want to purchase their items today and receive them yesterday.

Most times shipping goes smoothly, and items arrive on time, but there are many circumstances that are beyond your control, especially when you're dealing with international customers.

I normally post the following information in each of my listings and include it again in my shipping emails.

"Normal international delivery time is eight to fifteen business days, but it can take as long as four to six weeks—depending on customs and other shipping issues. Please be patient, and take this into consideration when placing your orders."

It helps to set buyer expectations before buyers place an order. That way if the customer asks where their item is you can refer them back to the info posted in your listing. By giving realistic delivery time frames upfront, you're going to save yourself a lot of grief and wasted emails trying to explain why customers haven't received their packages yet.

Remember—International customers have you over the barrel. Tracking is virtually nonexistent for international shipments. The post office is experimenting with international delivery confirmation to select countries, but the service is spotty at best. There's no guarantee the mailman in Canada or the UK will scan your package when he drops it off. He may be having a bad day, or he may be trying to outrun a dog. If your customer decides to file an item not received case you're going to lose because there's no way to provide proof of delivery.

Sorry to be the one to break it to you, but it's a fact of life when you are doing business on eBay. I've only had this happen once. A buyer in Germany opened an item not received case two days after paying for his item. There was no possible way it could travel from Iowa to Germany in two days.

Guess what? It didn't matter. eBay and PayPal decided the case against me because I didn't have proof of delivery. Like I said, this happened on out of five thousand international shipments, so it's not a big deal.

One other quick comment here—many sellers assume proof of shipping is enough to win an international case. It's not. A stamped customs form from your post office is of no help to you if the buyer files an item not received case. If you don't have proof of delivery, you don't have a leg to stand on.

List Your Items on International Sites

What we have talked about so far involves listing your items on eBay.com, and making them available to buyers in foreign countries. The reason this works is eBay.com is the largest of the eBay sites and has the most listings posted to it. As a result, many international buyers search here first when they're looking for new items.

If you do a lot of business with certain countries, you may be able to increase sales there by listing items directly on that site.

If you're a registered eBay user, you can sell on any of eBay's international sites. To get started just log in with your current ID and password, and start listing your items. Sellers with anchor stores can list on international sites for free. Sellers without an anchor store are charged listing fees if they exceed their free limits

If you want to make more sales, there are a few details you should consider.

1. What language are you going to post your listings in?

If you're selling in Canada, the United Kingdom, or Australia— English might be fine. But, the UK and Australia use different dialects, and the meanings of words are not always the same.

Canada has a large French speaking population, so you need to consider them, too. Should you post in English and French?

If you're posting your listing in Germany, France, or Japan—what do you do? Many of the buyers there speak English as a second language, but do you want to leave their understanding to chance?

It's a tough call. You can use Google Translate or Bing Translate to write your description. The translations are usually stilted, and hard to read. A better choice would be to find a native language translator on Fiverr or odesk. They would be able to provide you with a more accurate translation.

If you are selling low dollar value or one-of-a-kind items, the translation apps are going to be your most cost effective option. If you're setting up more expensive items you are going to sell over and over again; a good translator can help you create more professional sounding listings that will make more sales. Look at it as an investment in your success.

Other sellers choose to rely on translation apps that let potential buyers select the language they want to read the description in. eBay offers several of these apps that you can place in your item description. One app is called *One Hour Translation,* and the other is *Translation for Worldwide.*

2. What about your title? Are the keywords and the context the same in German, Spanish, and other languages as they are in the United States?

Do you know what terms someone in Germany would use to search for an iPad or a smartphone? When they're looking for a denim jacket, what other terms would they use to search for it?

Your title is how potential buyers discover your item. If you don't know the local dialect or slang, how do you know the best words to use in your title?

Go back to item one. A translator fluent in the native language would be able to write the most appropriate title for your item listings.

3. What are you going to charge for shipping?

Do you charge international rates, offer free shipping, or split it somewhere in the middle?

Shipping is a key ingredient in determining how successful you'll be at international selling. The good news is items just about always make it to their destination. The bad news is sometimes packages take forever to arrive at their destination.

When I listed items on the eBay.Uk site I marked my items up a bit and offered free shipping. A funny thing happened—most of my items ended up selling to my regular customers here in the United States. It wasn't quite what I expected, but sales did go up.

After a month I switched tactics and offered a low-cost international shipping option—five dollars, compared to the nine dollar rate I charged on eBay.com. Once I did that, I started getting more buyers from the U. K.

Joseph Dattilo, the founder of Virtualbotix, LLC, says –

"We offer USPS and UPS shipping providers and generally have First Class International, Priority International, Priority Express International, and UPS International as an option. Initially, we only had First Class International as an option but found that very few high-value items sold, and we were contacted by dozens of buyers who demanded that we make other methods available.

"Since offering USPS Priority Mail International and USPS Priority Mail expresses International we have seen a dramatic increase in sales of items whose value is greater than $100. The interesting thing is that the boost to sales occurred, but the use of these more expensive services is still rather rare.

The final takeaway is sellers can benefit from offering a larger variety of shipping options, even if their customers decide not to take advantage of them.

4. How are you going to approach delivery time?

Even if you explain your item ships from the United States, many buyers aren't going to understand. All they are going to see is that your item listed on their home site—eBay.uk or eBay.de.

Shipping time is a tough call with any international shipping method. A lot of my First Class shipments make it to Europe faster than they do across the state. Others seem like they get buried on the proverbial slow boat to China.

The problem is, as a seller, you have no way of knowing which packages are going to get tied up in customs. The best you can do is help to set reliable delivery expectations for your customers.

Offer your customers a variety of mailing options—First Class International, Priority International, and Priority Express International, then give them time frames for delivery using each service. Tell customers the longest it should take for items to deliver. Most often their package will arrive sooner, and customers will be delighted because the item delivered sooner than they expected.

5. Are you going to price your item in U S dollars, Pounds Sterling, or Euros?

If you're selling on eBay.uk or eBay.de and you price your item in dollars, it's going to confuse buyers. If you price your item in Pounds Sterling or Euros, you are going to have to keep a close eye on currency fluctuations to make sure you don't end up taking a bath if the market turns. When you go to pull your money out of PayPal, it's a two-step process. You have to convert your currency to U S dollars first, and then transfer funds to your bank account.

6. What are you going to tell your customers about VAT taxes, customs fees, and duty fees?

Customers aren't going to understand why they have to pay extra fees and taxes. When you list items on their home site, they don't associate the purchase triggering additional fees for customs and duty.

To prevent negative feedback and multiple returns you need to explain in every listing that your item ships from the United States and customers are responsible for all customs and duty fees as well as VAT taxes. You need to include the same information in every shipping email.

Joseph Dattilo, of Virtuabotix, says they adhere to eBay's policy on every international listing and include the following disclaimer in every item description –

"For international orders (outside of the United States of America) please allow for additional time for your products to arrive, or choose one of our expedited services to ensure your product arrives in a timely manner. Basic international shipping can take as much as 30 to 60 days depending on your country while expedited international shipments have guaranteed delivery windows.

"Import duties, taxes, and charges are not included in the item price or shipping cost. These charges are the buyer's responsibility.

"Please check with your country's customs office to determine what these additional costs will be before bidding or buying."

All sellers should include similar wording in their international listings. If you don't include similar wording, eBay may decide a case against you if a customer opens a buyer protection case against you citing extended delivery times or additional fees for customs.

Nick Vulich

Open an International eBay Store

If you're serious about international selling and have a target market in mind, it could make sense to open an international eBay store.

Let's say you are doing a booming business selling vintage concert t-shirts. Your two best international markets are Germany and the United Kingdom. You have just picked up a new line of custom printed t-shirts, hoodies, bikinis, and other apparel items. The new items are selling well to buyers who like the vintage look, but can't lay down several hundred dollars for a vintage t-shirt.

You know from experience the majority of customers who buy your vintage look apparel discover it in your eBay store. Sales in the U. K. and Germany aren't taking off, but your marketing intern had a light bulb moment—What if you opened local eBay stores in those markets so you could cross promote the vintage look apparel?

Bingo!

The best way to grow an international market is the same way you do it at home. Build an eBay store, and cross promote your items.

Set up a scrolling gallery at the bottom of every listing that features the vintage look apparel. Mention the vintage look apparel in every listing, and invite customers to explore your eBay store for more great deals.

Set up listing headers that feature the new items. Build a store front with clickable links to the new categories. Make it bold. Make it visual.

Use Markdown Manager to your advantage. Offer free shipping occasionally. Discount a different category every week or every month. Set up promotion boxes to highlight your specials.

If you are setting up an eBay store in a non-English speaking country, find a translator to set up your listings and titles.

....

An eBay store is a slightly more expensive way to sell international, but the payoff could be immense if you can make a go of it.

The key to success is to localize the store to each market you sell in, cross promote items as much as possible, and run frequent specials to build your brand.

Nick Vulich

Interview with Joseph Dattilo on International Shipping

(This is an extract of an interview with Joseph Dattilo of Virtuabotix. They sell on eBay, Amazon, and from their website https://www.virtuabotix.com/. Joseph is the founder of Virtuabotix, LLC, and handles much of the international selling for his company. His take on international selling should help both new and existing eBay sellers.)

Could you tell me a little bit about why you don't use the Global Shipping Program?

By the time the Global Shipping Program was a consideration we already had started shipping internationally from both Amazon and our Website. Because of the fees and other restrictions we opted to streamline shipping with our process.

One problem I've encountered with the program is sticker shock for my customers. When eBay includes their fees, shipping charges, customs, etc. the price is often three or four times what I normally charge. Is that similar to your findings?

In our experience the lower cost we can provide as an option for shipping, the more likely we will make the sale. Increasing the cost to international buyers did not seem like a viable strategy since we are able to maintain less than $10 shipping rates for basic international orders by shipping and insuring directly. Our estimates placed the cost at well around the 2 to 3 times mark if we used the Global Ship Program.

One concern everyone has is tracking with international shipments. What shipping services do you use? What has been your experience with tracking, or do you even worry about it?

We offer UPS and USPS shipping providers, and generally have First Class International, Priority International, Priority Express International, and UPS International as an option. Initially, we only had First Class International as an option. But we found very few high-value items sold. We were contacted by dozens and dozens of buyers who demanded we make other shipping methods available.

Since offering both USPS Priority Mail International and USPS Priority Mail Express International, we have seen a dramatic increase in sales of items whose value is greater than $100. The interesting thing is the boost to sales occurred, but the use of these more expensive services is still rather rare. Customers appear more likely to buy knowing they have the option to get it fast, but most still choose the most economical shipping method.

Even if you pay for tracking, a lot of times you can't track your packages. Priority Mail Express International is completely untrackable outside of the US (despite what is advertised by the postal service).

You mention international shipping is about 25% of your business? Are those numbers fairly consistent for you, or are they seasonal?

For our business there has always been a fairly large amount of international interest, so the ratio is fairly consistent regardless of time of year. The only time when that is not the case is during the holidays (October to January). US sales greatly increase on all channels during that period.

Which countries are your buyers coming from now?

Canada, Australia, and most of the Eurozone countries perform fairly well. There's also a strong market in Brazil, Chile, and several other South American countries.

It is likely that our sales in Spanish speaking countries would improve if we made a Spanish version of our listings available.

Do you use eBay's international visibility program, or do you just enable international shipping?

We simply enable international shipping at this point, and we seem to be selling well in international markets.

You said you also sell on Amazon and from your website. How do international sales from those sites compare to eBay?

International performance is very strong on eBay and Virtuabotix.com, especially when compared to Amazon. One reason for this is Amazon forces you to provide only two methods of international shipping. That means the only two options we can provide are standard, and the most expensive shipping option. This also makes it difficult to list things with LIPO batteries that have to have customized shipping rules and require UPS shipping (which is extremely expensive).

I know a lot of sellers who shy away from international shipping because of all of the horror stories they've heard about packages getting lost, stolen, etc. Do you have a big problem with international shipments going astray? Or are your numbers similar to those for domestic packages?

International orders and customers can be as difficult as the stories make them out to be—sometimes. And, there are some problem orders, but when you consider only 1 in 200 orders tends to have problems (caused by the post office), it's still a fairly good track record.

We used to have a lot more problems with international customers, but that was primarily due to poor communications, and customers not having clear delivery expectations. Some of the worst situations with international order disputes were because it was not clear how long standard orders can take to deliver. Delivery can take as long as 30 to 60 days (It's always better to overestimate).

An even worse problem is first-time international buyers who are outraged by having to pay VAT taxes and other import fees specific to their country.

To address a lot of those problems, we put the verbiage below to help. The part about import duties and taxes is required to be inside your listing verbatim to fit the guidelines eBay requires to remove negative feedback that specifically relates to VAT & other Taxes or duties.

International Buyers – Please Note:

For international order (outside of the United States of America), please allow for additional time for your products to arrive, or choose one of our expedited services to ensure your product arrives in a timely manner. Basic International shipping can take as much as 30 to 60 days depending on your country while expedited international shipments have guaranteed delivery windows.

Import duties, taxes, and charges are not included in the item price or shipping cost. These charges are the buyer's responsibility.

Customs Forms

The easiest way to handle customs forms is by using online shipping tools. When you use the online tools available through eBay, Click-N-Ship, Endicia, or Stamps.com, they automatically walk you through the forms and ensure they get filled out correctly.

For those of you who insist on doing it old style here's a quick tutorial on customs forms.

The post office uses two customs forms—Form 2976 and Form 2976-A. Form 2976 is required on all international packages weighing less than four pounds. Form 2976-A is required for all international packages weighing more than four pounds.

Form 2976

Form 2976

The key information needed for each form is –

- Sender's address
- Recipient address
- Value of each item enclosed
- Total value of all items enclosed
- Description of contents
- Sender's signature

You have several choices to describe the contents including gift, document, commercial sample, other. You need to check other, and then describe the contents in the description box.

Often sellers will ask you to lie about the value or check the gift box, so they don't have to pay duty fees (taxes). Be aware if you get caught doing this, it is a felony—subject to fines and jail time. If you're tempted to fudge the form for them, ask yourself—is the extra sale worth the penalties you could face?

That's pretty much all there is to it.

Have the post office walk you through your first customs form. After doing it once or twice, you'll be a pro and wonder why you ever worried about international shipping.

Form 2976 A

Form 2976A

Remember, form 2976 A is for international packages that weigh over four pounds or contain contents valued at over $400.

The key information needed to fill out form 2976 A is –

- Sender's address
- Recipient address
- Value of each item enclosed

- Total value of all items enclosed
- Description of contents
- Sender's signature

You have several choices to describe the contents including gift, document, commercial sample, other. You need to check other, and then describe the contents in the description box.

Know Your Numbers

(*Much of this section was originally published in my book -* **eBay Bookkeeping Made Easy**. *It's a primer on bookkeeping, taxes, business types, and tax deductions. The information in this section can save you thousands of dollars on your taxes every year.*)

Get Organized

The first thing you are going to need is a system to organize and store your receipts and records. Some sellers use a file cabinet. Some use expandable file folders. I like to use loose-leaf binders. I get a five-inch binder, monthly divider inserts, and storage pocket inserts.

Storing everything this way keeps all of my business records readily accessible, and the binder fits neatly on my bookshelf. I can store fifteen years of business records side-by-side in a relatively small space.

Save your receipts

Get used to it now. You need to save all of your receipts.

When you buy something online, print out the invoice, punch it with a three hole punch and store it in your three-ring binder under the month of purchase.

Save all of your mortgage or rent receipts, utility bills, phone bills, cable bills, sewer bills, etc. Store them in a zipper pouch in your binder. You're going to need them to file for the home office deduction. It's going to save your thousands of dollars on your taxes every year.

If you purchase supplies at Walmart, Staples, Office Depot, etc. save your receipts in a No. 10 envelope. Label the envelopes by month and store them in a zipper pouch in your binder.

Write down your mileage

Go to Walmart, Target, or your office supply superstore and buy a mileage log. They cost about three bucks and can save you close to a thousand dollars over the course of the year.

Starting today – You need to write down the beginning mileage on your vehicle. Every time you get in the car to run to the post office, pick up supplies, cruise a garage or estate sale, or anything related to your business – write it down. You need to record your beginning and ending mileage. Jot down a quick note about where you went, or why you went there. It doesn't have to be a novel or anything fancy. Post Office, Bank, yard sale – just something to leave a trail of how it was business related.

Save all of your auto-related receipts as well. The government lets you deduct your actual travel related expenses, or the mileage deduction (56¢ this year), whichever is greater. To ensure the largest deduction, you need to save your car payment stubs, insurance payment records, gas receipts, repair bills, oil change receipts, anything related to your car. Grab another No. 10 envelope for each month, and label it auto expenses.

Claim your workspace

To claim the home office deduction, you need to devote a portion of your home exclusively to your online business. Pick a room, a portion of a room, your garage, basement, or whatever. Get everything not related to your business out of there, and set up your workspace.

Even if you create most of your listings sitting in the recliner in front of the TV, you need a separate room for storage, mailing, and quiet time. The space your chair occupies doesn't count as a work area for the home office deduction, and neither does the kitchen table if it doubles as a shipping center and a suppertime smorgasbord.

Open a business checking account

You are running a business now. One of the first things you need to do is separate your business and financial expenses.

Open a business checking account, and get a business debit card and credit card. Having separate bank accounts does two things. In the case of an IRS audit, it shows them you are serious about your business. And two, it keeps you from nickel and diming your business to death. The minute you deposit your eBay money in your personal account you're going to start spending it on a Starbucks coffee, a Mickey D's burger, whatever. If you want to track your business earnings and expenses accurately, you need to separate it from your personal money.

PayPal is for business

Starting today, you need to decide that your PayPal account is a part of your business. Don't make personal purchases with your PayPal account. If you have a PayPal debit card, stop using it to buy pop, gas, groceries, etc. Use it for work related tasks like when you pick up shipping supplies or purchase inventory for your business.

When you do slip up and make a personal purchase with your PayPal account or PayPal debit card, make sure you label it as a personal expenditure. That way it won't mess with your accounting records.

Set aside money to expand your business

Once money starts pouring into your account, it's easy to get caught up in spending it. Decide up front to reinvest a certain percentage of your profits into expanding your business, whether that means adding new product lines, upgrading your computer system, or updating your work area.

Do this today, before the extra money becomes a part of your regular spending habits.

Make a plan, and work your plan

This one ties into setting money aside for business expansion.

After your business has been running for a while, it's time to sit down and develop a business plan. Decide where you want to be in six months, a year from now, and five years from now. It doesn't have to be a lengthy document. You can start by jotting down a few notes – I want to double my sales over the next eighteen months, or by this time next year I want to be making $20,000 a year.

As time goes, by change and refine your plan. Make it more specific. Make a list of short term and long term targets, and check them off as you reach them.

In short, make a plan, and work your plan.

....

Bookkeeping should be an important part of your plan. Numbers measure business success.

You don't need to be an accounting genius to be successful selling online, but you do need to know enough to understand your numbers.

In the next section, I'm going to give you a list of accounting terms that can come in handy. The more you understand them, the better you will be at managing your business.

Here's the very least you need to know about accounting to run your business properly.

Accounting records get recorded in what's called a **general ledger**. It is a financial record of a company over a period. The information recorded in it is used by accountants and accounting programs to prepare financial statements.

Accountants use what's called a double entry system. A debit on one side gets offset by a credit on the other side. The good news is with today's advanced software; business owners don't need to know anything about debits and credits. The program does all of the heavy lifting for you and crunches the numbers.

A **balance sheet** shows a company's assets, liabilities, and owner's equity at a given point in time. The simple formula behind the balance sheet is –

assets = liabilities + owner's equity

A **cash flow statement** shows all the money a company earns and spends over a period. Companies use cash flow projections to help manage their spending, and ensure they have the required money on hand to cover their bills.

A profit and loss statement or **P & L statement** shows whether a business is profitable or not over a period. Companies prepare P & L statements monthly, quarterly, and yearly.

The general format for the P & L statement is to list income accounts at the top, then expenses, followed by a final line that shows the "bottom line" – or profit and loss.

If you understand these reports, you will be more in tune with the financial health of your business.

GoDaddy Bookkeeping

GoDaddy Bookkeeping is available as an app you can download from eBay's applications bar. Amazon and Etsy sellers can check out the online version by visiting this link http://www.godaddy.com/accounting/accounting-software.aspx?isc=gooob012&ci=87249.

The service was originally known as Outright and was taken over by GoDaddy. It's an online accounting solution that will serve the needs of most users. It automatically imports transaction data from your PayPal account and posts it to the proper categories. Users can also sync their business credit cards and checking accounts with the service.

For sellers conducting business on multiple platforms, GoDaddy Bookkeeping can import transaction data from eBay, Amazon, and Etsy. It also works with several invoicing services including FreshBooks, Shoeboxed, and Harvest.

Here's the least you need to know. GoDaddy Bookkeeping is available on the *Applications* tab on your *My eBay* page. Hover your mouse over *Applications* until it shows Manage Applications, click on this and scroll through the list of applications until you come to *Outright*. Click on *Outright*, and select it.

GoDaddy Bookkeeping is available as a monthly ($9.99) or yearly ($99.00) subscription. Choose your poison and follow the prompts to get started.

Overview

The first page you see is your account overview. It contains all of the basic information about your account. In the upper right corner, it shows your yearly profit or loss so you can tell at a glance where you stand. Below this is a graph that charts your income and expenses, a pie chart that shows your current month's expenses, and then a list of open invoices.

Below this is a section that shows Invoice Activity. Most online sellers aren't going to use this feature as all of your invoicing is done through eBay, Amazon, Etsy, and your e-commerce storefronts. If you are running a side business where your customers pay through PayPal, this is where you would bill your customers for products or services sold.

In the left-hand column, you will see four small blue boxes. The first box is labeled *New This Week* and tracks your new sales and any uncategorized expenses. To view your new transactions or uncategorized expenses click on the number, and it will take you to your general ledger.

The *Money I Have Box* lets you view the balances in your accounts – PayPal, Amazon, and any bank accounts you have connected.

The Money I Owe box shows your liabilities or the money you owe. Some of the accounts shown here are your eBay balance, and money owed to Amazon and Etsy for seller fees.

The last box is labeled *Taxes*. It shows you several key tax indicators for your business. The first line shows your estimated quarterly tax payment, and when it is due. The mileage line shows your year to date mileage expenses. When you click on mileage, it takes you to your general ledger and lets you log your mileage. The last line shows your *Sales Tax Liability*, so you always know how much you owe.

Below the four blue boxes, you should see two blue bars. *Add Account* lets you add your various seller accounts, PayPal Account, and any bank accounts you want to tie into GoDaddy Bookkeeping. *Refresh All* imports data from your connected accounts so that you're viewing the most recent information available.

If you scroll back up to the top of the page, you will see your six control tabs – Overview, Income, Expenses, Reports, Taxes, and Manage. When you click on any of these, they open more program options.

Before I describe the control tabs, there's one other item I should cover. Sometimes a tan bar will appear just below the control tab. It shows program alerts or problems GoDaddy Bookkeeping may be experiencing with your account. When you click on the Fix It highlight, it will walk you through solving the problem so you can get your program up and running correctly again.

....

You can view your profit & loss statement anytime by clicking on the *view details* tab underneath where it says *(Year) Profit & Loss* on the GoDaddy Bookkeeping *Overview* page.

Your Profit & Loss statement gives you a quick overview of the financial health of your business. The top section shows your sources of income, and the bottom section details your expenses.

The final line shows your "bottom line," or the actual profit or loss your business is making.

The default view for your P & L is the previous twelve months, but you have the option to change that any time you would like. Scroll up to the top of the page under *Profit & Loss* where you see *ending*. You can choose the ending month or year, or you can change the period today, week, month, quarter, or year. To return to the chart select the chart icon on the right-hand side.

If you want to take a closer look at a transaction all of the items on your P & L are clickable. Select the one you want to examine, and it will take you to the general ledger page for that category.

At the bottom of the page, you will see two tabs at the far right side. Export lets you transfer P & L information to a Microsoft Excel file. Selecting print will give you a hard copy of your P & L.

Income

The income tab lets you manage your online income accounts. When you click on income, it takes you to your general ledger page for income, and you can view your most recent transactions.

Once again, all of the transactions displayed are clickable. If you want to edit a transaction, select it, and make the needed corrections.

What I recommend is to set up categories for all of your income transactions so you can track where your money is coming from. When GoDaddy Bookkeeping imports income transactions, it brings all of them in under the general "sales" heading. If you are just selling on one venue, such as eBay or Amazon, that's not a problem. If you sell across multiple platforms, it's important to know where your money is coming from. This way you can take corrective action if a sales venue is underperforming.

Every time you make a sale GoDaddy Bookkeeping records it as two separate transactions. The merchandise portion gets recorded under the "Sales" heading. If you charged postage on the transaction, it gets recorded under the heading "shipping income."

To add additional sales categories, select a transaction, and then scroll down the page until you see a heading labeled *Good to Know*. Over to the right-hand side, you will see a link labeled *Manage Categories*. Select it to see a chart of your current income categories. To add a category, select *New Income Category*. Categorize it as *Business* or *Nonbusiness*, and then name the new category. After doing this, you need to select a tax category. To tie the category you created to sales; you would choose *gross receipts or sales*. Select *create*, and your new category is ready to use.

To give you an idea of how to use this, I added the following categories to my income account – eBay sales, Amazon, Bonanza, *eBid*, bidStart, Kindle, Create Space, and Audible. By doing this, I can keep separate tabs on each of my sales channels. It gives me better control over my business and allows me to spot patterns early as they're beginning to emerge.

After you set up your income categories, you need to assign each transaction to the proper category. The easiest way to do this is from the Overview page. Select *view details* to see your P & L. Click on *sales* in the income section of your P & L. This will pull up all of your unassigned items. Select each item separately, and assign it to the proper income account. This step is pretty straightforward and should take just a few moments a day.

Whenever you're working on your P & L, you also want to take a look at your uncategorized expenses. They are listed at the bottom of the P & L, just before you see your bottom line. Most items are categorized when they get imported, but there are usually a few uncategorized items, either because you purchased from a new supplier and GoDaddy Bookkeeping doesn't know how to classify it, or because the items you purchased from that supplier may fit into several different expense categories. Click on the individual unclassified transactions and assign them to the proper category.

If you do this every time you open your program, it will only take a few minutes of your time, and it will ensure your P & L is up-to-date and accurate.

Expenses

When you select expenses, it brings up the general ledger view for your business expenses.

Similar to the income category, you can set up personalized categories to customize GoDaddy Bookkeeping for your business needs. Select an individual expense to enter the edit mode. Scroll down the page until you see the heading *Good to Know*. Move your mouse to the far right of the page and click on *manage categories*. Select *new expense category* and follow the prompts. Categorize the expense as a business or nonbusiness expense and name it. Scroll through the *tax category list* to tie your new expense to the proper category, and then select *Create*.

I would suggest setting up custom categories for your internet and cell phone providers, storage space rental, etc.

I find it useful to lump a few expense categories together. The main category I do this with is postage. I throw all of my shipping expenses in there – boxes, packing tape, stay free mailers, peanuts, you name it. The reason I do this is it makes it easier to compare my shipping expenses and shipping income. As long as the shipping income is equal to or more than my shipping expense, I know I'm on the right track. When they get out of whack, it's time for an intervention to determine what went wrong.

With my other expenses, my main concern is that they're consistent from month-to-month. If one month is way up without a similar bump in sales, it's time to investigate what happened. Sometimes it's a special purchase I had the opportunity to make; sometimes a number was entered wrong. The key is to watch your numbers and react when you see that something is out of whack.

Reports

When you select reports, it brings you to your Profit and loss statement. GoDaddy Bookkeeping always shows you the chart first. Select *view as a table* to see your P & L Statement.

If you are running a business, you should know these numbers forwards and backward. Growth is good, but I like to see consistent numbers across the board.

When I'm comparing my book sales numbers, the first thing I do is compare them with the last few months. If sales seem unusually low, I take a peek at last year's numbers to see if it's a seasonal trend. You should do the same thing.

Online sales are always slower in summer. They normally pick up by late August and run strong through spring. February is a little iffy – it can go either way. The first half of November can be the same way waiting for Christmas buying to kick in.

Key point: Use your P & L to help forecast fluctuations in your business. Study it for trends, where sales are increasing or decreasing, or where expenses are rising. Put on your detective hat and figure out what's happening. Doing this will make you a better business person, and help your business to grow stronger over the long haul.

Taxes

The taxes section helps you with three specific areas.

1) It provides your Schedule C information to make tax time a breeze. Just transfer over the numbers, and you're ready to file. Keep in mind; you're still going to need a tax advisor or a good tax program like TurboTax Business or HR Block Business. GoDaddy Bookkeeping doesn't figure the home office deduction, tax credits, etc. They just provide you with the raw numbers to fill out your Schedule C.
2) GoDaddy tracks your sales taxes due, so it's easy to file and submit your state reports. As long as you have eBay, Amazon, and Etsy set up to collect sales tax in your state, GoDaddy Bookkeeping will track all of the information for you.
3) Every time you log in, you can see your estimated tax payments and the date they are due. This way the due date and the amount you owe won't sneak up on you.

Manage

When you select manage it displays a list of all the accounts you have connected to GoDaddy Bookkeeping. If any of the accounts have errors, you will see a tan bar displayed by them. Click on the blue *Fix It* link to take care of account issues.

To connect more accounts, select *Add an Account* at the top of the page.

Good to know

You can easily reassign categories if something appears miscategorized.

Most often when this happens, it's because the program does not recognize how to classify the transaction. To fix the problem select the item that needs to be classified. At the far right, it will say the uncategorized item, select the correct category from the drop-down box, and press save.

You will also need to re-categorize items when you make a non-business related purchase. GoDaddy Bookkeeping has a *personal expense* category you can assign the item to so it is removed from your business records. If you sell a personal item and receive payment for an item through your PayPal account, you can reassign it to the *personal income* category.

Best advice

Keep a close eye on your accounting program. Update it every few days. It's easier to catch errors when just a few items are displayed. If you let it go too long, a large list of items to re-categorize can seem overwhelming.

Keep Records the Old-fashioned Way

What if you want to keep track of your income and expenses the old-fashioned way – using an Excel spreadsheet or a hand-written ledger?

No problem.

If you use Excel, you need to set up your income and expense categories the way accounting programs do. It should look something like this –

Income

- eBay sales
- Amazon Sales
- Etsy sales
- Bonanza sales
- bidStart sales
- Sales tax collected
- Shipping income

Expenses

- Cost of goods sold
- eBay fees
- Amazon fees
- Etsy fees
- Bonanza fees
- Internet expenses
- Phone
- Utilities
- Rent
- Computer equipment
- Software
- Professional fees
- Postage
- Mailing supplies
- Office supplies

Bottom Line

The easiest way to track your expenses is in a simple ledger style. Run your categories down the right-hand side of the page. Put your days across the top of the page. Leave room to subtotal your income and expenses. At the very bottom, you should have a space for your "bottom line" or profit and loss.

Assign a separate page for each month. At the end of each month transfer all of the information over to a page with yearly totals. Excel users have an advantage here because you can set these items to update automatically.

What I have outlined here is a very simple system, but it will give you all the information you need to manage your business. By looking at your income and expenses, you should be able to spot trends and identify cash flow problems.

The best advice I can give you is to try to update your information every day or two. If you let it go until the end of the month the task is going to seem overwhelming.

What You Need to Know About Taxes

Remember that old saying, "The only thing certain in life is death and taxes." Running a business is all about collecting and paying taxes.

Here are just a few of the different taxes you are going to be dealing with in your eBay business.

1) Sales & use taxes
2) Estimated taxes
3) Self-employment taxes
4) Unemployment tax
5) State and Federal Income Taxes

We are going to talk a little bit about each of these taxes – What they are? How they affect your business? And, what you need to do to stay on the right side of the IRS and your local tax authorities.

1) **Sales & use taxes**. Forty-five states require residents to pay a sales tax when they purchase property within that state. If you are an online seller and make a sale within your home state, you are required by law to collect the proper sales tax on it, and remit the payment to your state tax authority. Failure to collect sales tax

could put you on the wrong side of tax authorities if you get audited.

To collect taxes, you need to apply for sales and use tax permit (sometimes called a resale permit) from your state. There is normally no charge for it, but some states may require you to make a deposit based upon the volume of transactions you are expected to handle. It asks a few quick questions about your business, your sales channel, and your expected sales revenue. Once you receive your permit, you are required to collect tax on every transaction you process in your home state. Most states base your payment period upon your expected tax collections. As a result, you may have to remit payments monthly, quarterly, or annually.

Use tax is one of the most overlooked or misunderstood taxes. The way it's supposed to work is if you purchase something from outside of your home state and don't pay sales tax, you're supposed to fess up on your state income tax form and pay the appropriate tax. As you can probably guess, that rarely happens.

A good example of an item that would qualify for use tax is if you purchase your mailers from an out of state supplier on eBay. They ship them to you without charging sales tax. Because no sales tax was charged on this transaction when you purchased it, you are obligated to pay a use tax to make up for it.

The same thing is true for non-business owners. If you order clothes from a seller on eBay or Amazon and don't get charged sales tax, you are obligated to declare the transaction on your state income tax return, and pay the appropriate sales tax on it.

If you intend to purchase items from a wholesaler, they will require you to provide them with a state tax id. If you can't produce a tax id, some wholesalers will refuse to do business with you, others will insist on charging you sales tax on all of your purchases. You can also use your tax permit to eliminate sales taxes when you are purchasing items for resale from other retailers. So the next time you scoop up a cartload of closeouts at the outlet mall, you can save yourself a bundle by not having to pay the sales tax.

2) **Estimated taxes**. If you are self-employed, you are required to pay estimated taxes to the IRS and your state tax authority. Quarterly taxes are due April 15, July 15, October 15, and January 15. Tax programs such as TurboTax and H R Block will help you estimate your quarterly taxes. If you use GoDaddy Bookkeeping, it will show you your estimated taxes due. GoDaddy also shows your sales tax liability.

Keep in mind most of these programs estimate your taxes based on last year's income, or in the case of GoDaddy Bookkeeping, they base their estimates on your trending income. If your income is sporadic or changes from year to year, you may want to consult with an accountant or tax advisor to ensure you're paying the proper amount.

If you pay in less than a certain percentage of the amount that is due you may wind up having to pay extra fees and penalties.

3) **Self-employment taxes** are similar to Social Security and Medicare taxes charged to people who work for an employer. The only difference is self-employed persons need to self-report these taxes and pay both the employer's and the employee's share.

Self-employment taxes get figured on Schedule SE of your IRS Form 1040. In 2014 the self-employment tax rate was 15.3% - 12.4% for Social Security, and 2.9% for Medicare. In 2014 the amount of income subject to the portion of Social Security tax was capped at $117,000. There is no cap for the Medicare tax portion of self-employment tax.

You can deduct the employer portion of your self-employment tax (approximately 50 percent) when you figure your adjusted gross income for Federal taxes.

4) **Unemployment taxes**. If you hire employees to work in your online business, you are required to pay unemployment taxes. These vary by state. Just keep in mind, there is a separate state and Federal tax due.

See Publication 926 for more information and a list of state taxing authorities. http://www.irs.gov/publications/p926/index.html

5) **Federal and state taxes**. When most online sellers think about taxes, these are what come to mind.

Some online sellers try to avoid paying income taxes on their earnings or think taxes just for big time sellers. The truth is if you make as little as one dollar selling online you are required to report it for income tax purposes.

To keep everyone honest, the government imposed mandatory reporting requirements upon PayPal. If more than $20,000 gets deposited into your PayPal account during the year, PayPal is required to report it to the IRS on form 1099-K.

To view your form 1099-K sign into your PayPal Account, hover your pointer over the **history** tab, and this will bring up a drop-down menu. You want to click on **tax documents**, and this will give you the option to view a PDF file of your 1099-K if one generated for you.

You are not required to submit the PayPal 1099-K with your income tax filing, but you should be sure you are reporting at least as much income as is shown on it. You can be sure the IRS is matching them up, and taking a close look at your 1099-K, and the income you report on your tax return.

....

That's the very least you need to know about taxes and your online business. Here are a few more tips that can help you out when the time comes to prepare your Federal and state tax forms.

Business income gets reported on Schedule C of your Form 1040.

Several tax programs are available to make filing your business taxes easier. The two I've had the most experience working with are TurboTax Business and H R Block Premium or H R Block Premium & Business. Each of these programs will conduct a fact-finding interview with you about your business, and walk you step-by-step through filing your tax return.

If you pay extra for the premium version of GoDaddy Bookkeeping, it will generate a paper version of your Schedule C with all the information you need to key into your 1040 Tax Form. One other quick tip. If you don't pay for the premium version of GoDaddy Bookkeeping all of your information previous to the current twelve months will be hidden from your view. To ensure you don't lose any important financial data print a copy of your P & L, and your monthly statements before the end of January. If you don't, you will need to subscribe to the premium version to recover your information.

Even if you use an accountant or tax preparer doing your taxes first can save you hundreds of dollars when it comes time to file your taxes. This way all of the information is gathered together and entered in the correct areas on your tax return. All your tax professional needs to do is review everything to make sure there was nothing you overlooked or left out.

Most Common Tax Deductions

One of the perks of being a business owner is the ability to shift some of your income by taking advantage of various business deductions. Here are some of the most common business deductions taken by online business owners.

Home Office Deduction. Many business owners are afraid to claim the home office deduction because they have heard the IRS targets filers who take it. That's pretty much one of those urban legends that get bigger every time it's told.

The home office deduction is every online seller's best friend and can save you thousands of dollars on your taxes if you use it properly.

Here are the IRS rules for taking the home office deduction:
1) Your home must be your principal place of business.
2) You must use the area of your home (a room, or portion of a room) exclusively to conduct business. If you do all your work at your kitchen table, you don't qualify for the home office deduction because you don't use that area exclusively for business. If, on the other hand, you devote an extra bedroom, basement, or garage exclusively to conducting the activities of your online business—this space would qualify for the home office deduction.

To learn more about the home office deduction you can check out Publication 587.

http://www.irs.gov/publications/p587/index.html

The methods for calculating the home office deduction change frequently, so even if you have taken it in the past, you may want to brush up on the new guidelines.

Mileage Deduction. If you use your vehicle while conducting your business, you can deduct your expenses. Business owners can take either the standard mileage deduction or deduct the actual expenses incurred for the use of the vehicle in their business.

To take the mileage deduction, you need to record all the miles your car is driven for personal and for business use. I would recommend purchasing a mileage log. You can find one in the office supply section at Walmart or Target, or at larger office supply stores such as Office Max, Staples, or Office Depot. They run about $3.00 and are small enough to slip under your visor or into your glove box.

Each time you head to the post office, run to the store for mailing supplies, or to a yard sale or estate sale to pick up new inventory make sure to record your beginning and ending mileage.

In 2016, the standard mileage deduction was 54¢ per business mile driven, down from 57.5¢ in 2015. If you opt to deduct actual expenses, make sure to record all of your expenses for car payments, insurance, repairs, tires, oil changes, and gasoline. You can then deduct the percentage of expenses based on the miles driven for business usage.

Travel. Did you ever want to visit California or Hawaii, but weren't sure you could afford it?. The cost of travel is fully deductible if it is business related.

Let's say you are ready for a vacation and eBay is throwing a seller get together in Scottsdale. You can deduct all of your expenses – airfare, car rentals, cabs, motels, food, and admission – as long as they are related to the event. If your spouse helps out in your business, their expenses are covered as well. If you decide to make a real vacation of it and bring the kids along too, you would not be able to deduct expenses for their travel, food, lodging, etc. if they do not participate in the business.

The travel expense deduction can also be used to cover day trips out of town. If you visit an estate sale or auction several hundred miles away, all your expenses related to the buying trip would be deductible. Again, if you bring along the kids or someone unrelated to your business, their expenses would not be covered.

Computers, printers, office supplies. Are you a techie? Have you always wanted to own the latest, greatest gadgets, but wished you had a rich uncle to help you out with the payments?

Uncle Sam can come to the rescue here too. You can deduct the price of a new computer, printer, cell phone, iPad, or any other gadget that you regularly use in your online business. The only hitch is the item needs to be for your business use only.

You have the option of depreciating the expense of your purchase over the expected life of the item, or in most cases, you can deduct the full value of the item.

Internet, cell phone, etc. If you purchase a separate cell phone or internet service for your business you can deduct the full cost of them as a business expense. If you use them for business and personal use, you can only deduct the portion of the service you use for business.

If you're on track to make a little too much money this year and are worried about paying extra taxes, look at some of these ideas as ways to shift your tax burden. Once again, don't go crazy. Before you rush off on that junket to Hawaii or Europe, consult with your tax advisor first to ensure the trip is deductible in your situation.

....

Here are two other suggestions while we're talking about tax deductions. You can use your business income to help fund your retirement or to shift money to your kids by employing them to work in your business.

When you own your own business, you can fund a personal retirement account, 401K, SEP IRA, or KEOGH. The individual details are beyond the scope of this book; consult a tax professional for more details.

If you have kids, put them to work for your company and pay them the money you would have given them anyway. If you have college-age kids, this is a good way to help them pay their way through college while deducting the expense from your business. Keep in mind when you do this it is just like hiring a regular employee. You need to pay unemployment taxes and provide a W-2 at the end of the year.

Business Permits, Licenses, and Such

Most eBay sellers run their businesses out of their homes. Their neighbors don't know anything about it, except for the frequent comings and goings of the mail trucks, UPS vans, and Fed Ex guys.

As such, most eBay sellers don't bother with licenses or permits. They go about their daily routine pretty much unaware they may be breaking local codes and regulations.

What I'm going to do here is talk a little bit about the different licenses and permits a typical eBay business owner might bump up against, and give you a few tips on how to get them.

DBA (Doing Business As). If you conduct your business using an assumed (fictitious) name you are required to record your information with the city clerk's office or county clerk's office depending on where you live. Sometimes you can fill out the form online. Other times you will be required to go to the appropriate office, and pay a small fee. They check to see if the name is in use by another company. If it is, you need to pick a new name. Banks will require a copy of your DBA if you attempt to open an account in your business's name.

Business License. Most cities and counties require a license to conduct business within their boundaries. The fees vary based on the type of business you run. Where I live you apply for a license with the city's department of revenue. If you are unsure where to apply for a business license in your area Google "city name business license."

EIN (Employer Identification Number). Most online businesses conduct their business using the owner's social security number. If you prefer not to share that information you can apply to the IRS for an EIN. Here is a link to apply for an EIN online https://www.us-tax-id-number.com/?gclid=CJaB3Kq_jr4CFckWMgod63cAbQ.

Home Business Permit. Some municipalities require homeowners to register if they are conducting business out of their home. Call your city clerk's office to learn more about your areas licensing requirements.

Sales & Use Tax Permit. If you make sales to residents within the boundaries of your state, you will be required to collect sales tax. Contact your state department of revenue for more information.

The SBA offers an excellent website covering local business licenses that may be required. They even have a search feature where you can enter your zip code, and it will return a list of business licenses and permits you may require. Follow this link for more details http://www.sba.gov/licenses-and-permits

Choose Your Business Structure

How you structure, your business plays a key role in how much money you will keep at the end of the year.

Most eBay businesses will take one of the following structures.

1) Sole proprietorship
2) Partnership
3) Corporation
4) Small business corporation (Subchapter S)

Sole proprietorship

A sole proprietorship is the simplest form of business entity. One person runs it with no distinction between the individual and the business. If the business makes money, you keep all of the profits. If the business loses money, you are responsible for all of the losses.

Most sole proprietorships are conducted using the business owner's name. If you choose to run it under a different name you may need to file a DBA (Doing Business As). Normally, you would need to register your business with the City Clerk's Office or a county office and pay a small fee. They will check to see if the name you want to use is already in use. If another business is using it, you will need to choose another name.

Your business income should be recorded on Schedule C of your IRS 1040 tax form and would get taxed at your normal rate.

The major disadvantage of a sole proprietorship is you are 100% responsible for business liabilities. If you sell defective products or someone gets hurt on your business premises, you are fully responsible and could get sued for liability.

Partnership

A partnership is a business relationship between two or more people. Partners normally sign a partnership agreement. Each of them contributes a certain amount of capital and labor, and shares in the profits or losses of the business.

Partners can share equally in the profits, or certain partners may have a larger percentage of ownership based upon the partnership agreement. Income gets reported to each partner on a form called a Schedule K-1.

The disadvantage is partners are fully responsible for any liabilities contracted by the business.

Corporation

A corporation is an independent legal entity owned by its shareholders. The business gets registered with the State Corporation Department or Secretary of State's Office. They are required to have business licenses and permits, and to file quarterly and annual reports with the state they are incorporated in.

Corporations are normally owned by a large number of people who have issued shares in exchange for investing capital in the business.

Shareholders in the corporation receive income in the form of dividends. The biggest advantage of a corporation is income gets taxed at a lower corporate rate, and liability is limited to the money you have invested in the corporation.

Subchapter S Corporation

Subchapter S corporations pass earnings and losses through to shareholders for federal tax purposes. Shareholders report income on their personal tax returns and pay taxes at their normal rate.

To qualify as an S Corporation, the corporation must file Form 2553 Election by a Small Business Corporation. http://www.irs.gov/pub/irs-pdf/f2553.pdf

S Corporations have many advantages that make them attractive to online business owners.

1) Your assets are protected. The most you can lose as an investor is the money you have invested in the corporation.
2) Ability to reduce self-employment tax liability by paying yourself a portion of income as salary and as dividends.
3) Pass through taxation which allows owners to report losses or earnings on their personal tax returns.
4) It opens new possibilities in offering yourself corporate perks such as better retirement plans, writing off college expenses, and other benefits. Be sure to consult with a

qualified tax advisor before implementing any of these ideas.

Most online businesses begin life as a sole proprietorship and scale up as the business grows.

Nick Vulich

Sell your Stuff Off eBay

For most sellers, eBay is the place to cut your teeth in online selling. The site is easy to use, they have a built-in base of nearly 150 million eager buyers, and it's relatively inexpensive to get started.

The big four alternatives to selling on eBay are –

1. Amazon
2. Etsy
3. Fiverr
4. Personal website

Which one is the correct choice for your business depends on what you sell, your sales volume, and your business goals?

If you sell any products, Amazon is the clear choice for where to start selling next. If you sell handmade crafts or crafting supplies, Etsy would be a good choice. If you sell services such as eBook covers, website design, whiteboard videos, etc. Fiverr is a solid choice.

A personal website makes a good addition to selling on the above e-commerce sites, but as a standalone sales solution—it's not a good choice for most sellers.

The reason is the big e-commerce sites allow you to tap into their built-in customer base and reach hundreds of millions of ready customers; a personal website is only as strong as your mailing list.

If you're just starting out, that can be as few as ten or twenty customers.

Nick Vulich

Sell it on Amazon

Amazon is the proverbial 800-pound gorilla when it comes to e-commerce. Every online marketplace is trying their damnedest to emulate Amazon's success.

Unlike eBay and many other online commerce sites, Amazon doesn't charge separate listing fees for the items you put up for sale there. Sellers can add thousands of items to their Amazon store without putting up a penny until they sell something.

Another great thing about selling on Amazon is you can list most of your items in one minute or less. There's no need to snap any pictures or write a detailed item description. Selling your item on Amazon is as simple as hitching a ride on the Amazon listing page.

It's easy to spot the items listed by individual sellers. When you see a box like the one below, the items being sold by Amazon are listed under the Amazon price. The items offered by individual sellers are in the next two categories—used and new.

What I want to do first is take a minute to walk you through listing a typical item for sale on Amazon. Then I will come back and give you some pointers about how you can maximize your sales there.

Listing your first item on Amazon

Type the name or description of the item you want to sell into the Amazon search bar. Click on the item you want to sell. Off to the right-hand side, you will see a small box labeled **more buying choices**. At the bottom of this box click on the **Sell on Amazon** button.

At this point, you're eight steps away from listing your item for sale on Amazon.

Step 1. Amazon shows you the title and picture of the item you selected and asks you to verify this is the correct item you want to sell. If it is the correct item, you don't need to do anything.

Step 2. Tell people the condition of your item. Click on the radio button in the box labeled **condition,** and select the one that best describes the condition of your item.

Below this, you have a chance to add a comment about the condition of your item. If you are selling a textbook, you could say "overall very good condition, but it does have some highlighting in the first three chapters."

Step 3. Amazon shows you the lowest price listed for your item. Next, it shows the lowest shipping price available for it. What you're going to find, especially if you are selling new items, is Amazon has the lowest price, and shipping is free (with Amazon prime). Don't panic! People will still buy from you, even if you have a higher price, and charge shipping.

Step 4. Enter your selling price. Next, to the box where you enter your selling price, Amazon will show how much they are going to charge your customer for shipping.

Step 5. Tell Amazon how many of this item you have available for sale.

Step 6. This step tells Amazon to collect taxes if you have enabled them to do so. Casual sellers can skip this step.

Step 7. Enter your SKU (short for stock keeping unit). It's how you identify the item you are listing for sale. During my peak selling period, I had over 10,000 items listed for sale on Amazon. All of them were numbered and stored on storage shelves. Whenever one of them sold, I could go to that shelf, and easily pull the item for shipping.

When you're just starting out an SKU doesn't seem all that important, but if you intend to grow your business, you need to start thinking about some labeling system as early in the game as possible. It will keep you from having to backtrack or rework your listings down the road.

If you decide not to enter an SKU, Amazon will assign one for you.

Step 8. Select your shipping methods. Amazon requires you to add a basic shipping service. I would suggest choosing Expedited Shipping (priority mail), and the first international shipping option (first class).

Press the yellow **Continue** button at the bottom.

Review your selling information. The last few boxes show you Amazon's commission when your item sells, how much Amazon allows you for shipping, and how much money you will receive (including your shipping credit) after Amazon's commission is taken out.

If everything looks good, press the **Submit your listing** button.

The next thing you're going to see is **Congratulations! You've successfully listed _____.**

That's it. Your item is live on Amazon.

Sit back and wait for the sales to start rolling in, or better yet, list more items so you can make more sales.

That's all there is to selling on Amazon.

Add an item to the Amazon catalog

If you sell unique items that aren't already in the Amazon catalog, Amazon lets you add item description pages to their catalog. While it's not hard to do, it does take a little extra time and effort, so I'm going to cover this in more detail.

To add an item to the Amazon catalog you need to visit <u>Seller Central</u> and hover your mouse over **Inventory**. At the drop down menu select **Add a Product**.

Check the Amazon catalog to see if it is already listed. If your item is not currently available on Amazon, you can add it by clicking, **Create a new product**.

Select a category. To do this, you can either search for a category or browse through a list of categories. Choose the category that most closely fits your item.

After you select the category, you want to list your item in you will be taken to the sell your item dashboard.

The trick here is to provide as much information as you can under each of the six tabs you see at the top of your dashboard. Try to fill in every box you can, because Amazon will use the information you give to show your item in relevant search requests.

At the very least, you need to fill in the boxes with a red star to the left of them.

Vital Info. What you put here is going to become the title for your listing. Make sure it is keyword rich and describes your item properly. You have 250 characters to get it right and let potential buyers know what you're selling. Make the most of it. Give the name, manufacturer, model number, color, accessories, and other important information.

Manufacturer is what it says. If you know who made your item, list it here. If you know the brand name, enter it in the next line. Enter the model number and manufacturer number if they are available. Package quantity means how many of them are packaged together – one, two, or a dozen. The UPC or EAN are the manufacturer's product code. If you know the UPC code, enter it here.

Offer. List your selling price. Below that, you can create a sale price. If you enter a sale price, select when you would like the sale to run. Enter how many items you have. If you have a sales tax permit, enter the pertinent tax info so that Amazon can collect sales tax from your buyers.

Handling time refers to how many days it will be before you ship the item. Amazon's default is one or two days. If you need a longer lead time, specify it here. An example would be if you are working with a drop shipper, and it takes some time for the order to process through their system.

Selling date is the day you want Amazon to start showing your item. Gift options. Will you gift wrap the item, or include a card with it? Select the services you wish to offer. Restock date means if you are out of stock, when will more be available.

Import designations specify country of origin. Several choices are available. Read through, and choose the one most appropriate for what you are selling.

Next, you need to choose your shipping method. You can choose to ship the item yourself or to offer Fulfillment by Amazon (FBA). FBA means you shipped your products to Amazon when you listed them, and Amazon is handling shipping and fulfillment for you. The biggest advantage here is your items often qualify for Amazon's free shipping offers including those with Amazon Prime. Another advantage is many buyers are more comfortable buying from you because your item ships to them directly from Amazon.

I will talk about Fulfillment by Amazon, and how it can help to increase your sales, in more detail later in this chapter.

Images. You need to include at least one photo of your item. The more pictures you include, the easier it is to sell your item. Picture requirements are listed next to the uploading tool.

When you get your pictures ready to upload, you should keep in mind:

- Only show the exact item you are selling. Don't include any extra items or props in your pictures.
- Watermarks are not allowed.
- You cannot superimpose any text over your images.

- Your main image must be a photo. Drawings are not allowed.
- All pictures should be a minimum of 1000 x 500 pixels. Buyers cannot zoom in on smaller images, so they will not have close-up views of what you are selling.
- J-Peg illustrations are the preferred file type.

Description. The description section is broken down into two sections. One is for product features, and the next section is for your actual written description of the item.

Features provide bullets, loaded with bite-size information about your item. Here are some of the features given for the Apple iPad to give you an idea what type of features you should list with your items:

- Apple's newest generation of iPads
- 9.7 inch (diagonal) LED Glossy back-lit screen
- Forward facing and rear cameras
- Apple IOS 10 and access to Apple Apps store
- 1 GHz dual-core Apple A5 custom-designed processor

Your description should be feature and benefit rich. Write it in a narrative style. Everything should be product focused. Amazon doesn't allow you to include any information about your business.

After you list your item, the item description page becomes part of the Amazon catalog. Any seller with the same item can list it alongside yours on the same item description page.

Keywords. Keywords are tags you can add to your items to help buyers find them in search.

Search terms are where you enter the keywords buyers use to search for your item. Include all the obvious ones: Product name, model #, manufacturer, color, and size. If you are unsure which keywords to use, check the Google Keyword Tool. It will help you pick keywords people use to search for your item.

Try not to use single word search terms. Use "long tail keywords" whenever possible. Long tail keywords are more specific in nature and encompass most of the searches made on Google. Some examples of long tail keywords are: "Space exploration in the Milky Way Galaxy," "How to write better keywords," and "How to make money on Kindle."

More Details. This section lets you add more product specific information about your item. Some of the categories include: Brand, MSRP, Part number, model number, is your item subject to prop. 65 reporting in California, shipping weight, product and shipping size specifications, and the like. Specific information asked for is based on the type of product you are selling.

Press **save and finish**. In no time at all, your item will be live on Amazon.

It sounds complicated, but after you have added two or three products to the catalog, it will be a whole lot easier.

The biggest problem I have when I add custom pages is there's no real-time preview like you have on eBay. It can take a half hour or more for the listing page to display on Amazon, so you need to check back later to make sure everything posted okay. Another problem when you are adding pictures is it can take ten or fifteen minutes for them to upload, so you are stuck waiting before you can work on your next product listing.

If you have a large catalog of items, you can upload them through a spreadsheet. There are also services that help eBay sellers move their entire eBay store to Amazon.

One service I have had experience with is [Export Your Store]().

What I like about using Export Your Store is they do all the heavy lifting for you as far as moving your items from eBay to Amazon. The bad thing about using Export Your Store is Amazon is nothing like eBay. After they transfer your items to Amazon, you need to optimize everything for selling on Amazon.

Here are a few of the differences between eBay and Amazon that can cause you problems.

- Amazon is a marketplace. They don't allow personal branding or HTML code in any of their item description pages.
- Amazon doesn't allow references to your business in their item description pages.
- Amazon requires tags (keywords) to be entered in the proper section of their listing form to help buyers find your item in search.

The folks at Export Your Store are really good at stripping the HTML code out of your listings, and getting them moved over to eBay. I had over ten thousand items exported from eBay to Amazon in just over two days.

Then I started receiving a stream of item violation warnings from Amazon. When I imported my eBay items, you could still have your customer service email address in your listings. This violated Amazon's terms of service, so I was forced to go through just over 10,000 items, one at a time, and edit each of them individually.

What followed was three weeks of pure hell, spending twelve to fourteen hours of every day, checking, revising, and deleting listings.

A few other things I discovered while editing my listings was sometimes when they stripped out the HTML code from my listing templates; they also removed part of my item descriptions including the SKU numbers I used to locate items once they sold. I had to add keywords to every single Amazon listing (I think this was because I sell one of a kind collectibles, and each item required adding a new page to the Amazon catalog). If you are selling more traditional items, like electronics, books, CD's, or DVD's that already have a catalog page, this would not be an issue.

Despite all the problems I mentioned, I would still recommend Export Your Store. Customer service was responsive, and they worked quickly to resolve my problems. The current charges for exporting your eBay store to Amazon start at $99 for the first 1,000 items and work up to $249 for up to 15,000 items. These are per month fees that keep your inventory and prices synched between the two sites.

Several other companies can help you export your eBay store items to Amazon. Two of them are Vendio and Linnworks.

Amazon FBA

Amazon FBA (Fulfillment by Amazon) can help skyrocket your sales. Sixty-four percent of people who have used Fulfillment by Amazon have increased their sales by 20% or more.

When you use Fulfillment by Amazon, Amazon becomes customer service central for your business.

Here are the top benefits you receive by using FBA:

- Your items become eligible for FREE Super Saver Shipping and Amazon Prime Benefits,
- Your FBA items are displayed with no shipping charges, giving you the benefit of being a lower priced seller.
- Your back end is taken care of by Amazon. They handle all the shipping, returns, and customer service problems for you.
- Your items become eligible to compete for the Buy Box.

By using FBA, you free up more of your time to source new products, and to enjoy life more.

You ship your inventory to Amazon's warehouse. Once they check your items in and receive them into their inventory, they go live on Amazon. Each time one of your items sells, you will see it show up in your seller dashboard, but the good folks at Amazon do all the heavy-lifting for you. They collect your payment. They ship the order for you, and they handle all customer service issues or returns.

Compare that with being an eBay Top-Rated Seller who is required to ship their item with a one-day handling time to receive their 20% final discount fee. The eBay seller is chained to his computer, while the Amazon FBA seller is free to enjoy his life without the constant rush to ship and handle customer service issues.

FBA is also a great deal for Amazon buyers.

FBA assures customers a great experience when buying from you. Most of the items sold through FBA are eligible for Amazon Super Saver Shipping, and other Amazon Prime Benefits, including free shipping on orders over $49.00 ($25.00 for qualified books).

Getting started with FBA

To get started using FBA:

- List your items in seller central, and select Fulfillment by Amazon as your shipping choice.
- If you already have the item for sale on Amazon, go to **Manage Your Inventory** on your Seller Central Dashboard. Select the product that you want to include as FBA.
- Print the labels provided by Amazon to ship your items to their warehouse.
- After Amazon receives and scans your items into their inventory, they go live and are ready for sale.

FBA Fees

For more detailed information on FBA fees, you can visit the Fulfillment by Amazon Guide. (These prices are current as of 12/01/2016. Be sure to check with Amazon for the most current prices.)

The very least you need to know is:

- There are pick and pack fees of $1.00 per item.
- There is a fee by weight starting at .47 per pound. Amazon charges a storage fee based on the cubic feet taken up by your items.

The fee is 54¢ per cubic foot from January to October, and $2.25 from November to December.

Sell it on Etsy

Etsy is a community of crafters who get together to buy and sell handmade items. Sellers can also offer craft supplies and certain vintage items.

A visit to the Etsy home page reveals several subtle differences compared to eBay and Amazon. Etsy has all the normal product pictures towards the top of the home page.

Below that are three featured Etsy *shops worth exploring.* Today's featured shops are RVS handcrafted, Fabric Shoppe, and Gretade Parry Design. A quick click on any of the pictures takes you to the Etsy shop. Gretade Parry Design is a perfect example of personal branding. The banner features three pictures of Gretade working on her products. Below that, you'll see another picture of Gretade in her work apron, followed by her product listings. Very nice.

As you scroll further down the page, you will find a link to several featured sellers, along with a blog post featuring the seller, their family, and some of the products they sell.

Today's featured seller is Kathleen Smith, and her husband Justin, better known on Etsy as Smiling Tree Toys. After you click on the link, it takes you to a photo interview loaded with pictures of Kathleen, Jeff, and their children, who are pictured making some of their custom wooden toys.

Just below this is a clickable banner; that asks, "What is Etsy." Want to know more? Just click on the link, and it'll explain everything.

The site has a folksy, down-home feeling, and it pervades the everything you see on Etsy. It's friendly, inviting, and both, buyer and seller oriented – Something eBay used to be back in the day before they started kissing up to the big sellers.

Etsy's focus is on helping artists, crafters, woodworkers, and other makers of handmade items sell their wares. Sellers are also able to offer crafting supplies, and vintage items if they are over twenty years old.

Getting started

To get started look for the big red button that says Etsy in the upper left-hand corner. Click the gray button next to it that says **register** and fill in the required information.

As with all e-commerce sites, the most important decision to make when you register is your username.

I encourage you to take some time on this. Your name should tell people a little bit about your business, and the type of products you sell. Many people on Etsy choose to use their name, and that's fine, too. On Etsy, your brand is all about you, and the products you make.

Once you sign up, you should fill in your profile so buyers can get to know you better. In the upper right corner, you should see a link that says **Hi username**. Click on that. It will bring you to Etsy's profile page. Click where it says **edit profile**.

The first thing you should do is add a profile picture. I suggest a photo of you, surrounded by some of your crafts, or of you working on a project. If you are feeling a little shy and don't want to include yourself in the picture, pick one of your favorite projects and upload a picture of it.

Continue filling out this form. Add as much information as you can. If you want to change your username, you can change it here. The last few lines at the bottom of this section let you select where you would like to share your profile information. By default, Etsy puts a check by these, so your profile information will show up in as many places as possible. Uncheck any information you would rather not share.

Over to the right hand, side of the screen you will see your control panel. Click on settings, and continue adding information to your profile.

- **Account**. If you have a Facebook or Twitter account, you can link them to your Etsy account here. You can also update your email address, password, or close your account.
- **Preferences** allow you to set contact information and other such info from Etsy. Use this area to set your location and currency preference. At the top, you can choose to filter out mature (XXX) items so that they won't show up in your search results. Etsy has them filtered out by default, so you need to turn them on if you wish to receive mature selections.
- **Privacy** allows you to select who can see your favorites, and if people can search for you by your email address or not.

- **Security** gives you additional methods to help secure your account online. All of them are switched off by default, and you must manually turn them on.
- **Shipping address** is just what it says. Enter your full mailing address here.
- **Credit cards** lets you put a credit card on file with Etsy.
- **Emails** allow you to select your email settings, and what emails you would like to receive from Etsy, and from your customers.

The next section is **Apps**. As business picks up remember to buzz back here now and then, and download apps to help you grow your business.

Here are a few apps I've had the chance to try out. They will give you an idea of what's out there:
- Fanpageology: When Etsy Meets Facebook
- Etsy8: An app for Windows 8
- Pict is an app that allows you to snap a picture, share it with your social network, and sell.
- EtsyFu an app that allows you to schedule Twitter posts to promote your business
- Direct Mail Manager for Etsy

Make sure you bookmark this page. It is loaded with useful tools you can integrate into your Etsy business.

If you have a website, there's a cool tool named **Etsy Mini** that lets you build a widget so you can sell your Etsy items on your website.

Fees

Etsy fees are inexpensive and easy to understand. There is a listing fee of .20 for each item, and they run for four months. When your item sells, you pay a 3.5% final value fee.

At the end of the month, you receive a bill for your fees. All payments are due by the 15th of the month.

What's nice is the good folks at Etsy haven't raised their selling fees in at least the last three years that I've been selling there. Take that, eBay and Amazon.

Etsy Shop

All sellers can open an Etsy Shop. Your shop is your personal spot on the Etsy where you can brand yourself and your business. Etsy has a guide to help you get started. Click here to see the shop manual. http://www.etsy.com/help/article/246?ref=help_home

You should also visit the seller handbook. Click here to see it. http://www.etsy.com/blog/en/category/seller-handbook/

The manual does a good job of walking you through setting up and customizing your Etsy Shop.

Follow these steps to set up your shop:

- **Give your shop a name.** Remember what we said earlier. Make it unique, and make sure it describes your business. Barring that, use your name.
- **Upload a banner** to customize your shop further. Picture requirements are 760 x 100 pixels. If you are unsure where you can get a banner made, Fiverr has some great designers. They have a lot of designers that will make you a fantastic banner starting at $5.00.

- **Add a shop announcement**. The first 160 characters of your shop announcement are what show up in search when people search for your item using Google, Yahoo, and Bing. Make it short, descriptive, and compelling, so it will entice searchers to click on your shop.
- **Add shop sections**. This section is similar to categories in an eBay store. You can add ten sections to call out different product lines, items, or sizes.
- **Add shop policies**. Share information with your customers about how you do business. The main thing to remember is to keep your messages customer friendly. Too many sellers use strings of negatives words like "I don't," "I won't, "Checks and money orders will not be accepted."

It's ok to say what you will, and won't do, but say it nicely. People don't like it when you tell them what they can and can't do. They like to hear "this is what we can do for you."

Specific policies you can include are Welcome Message, Payment Policy, Shipping Policy, Refund Policy, Additional Information, and Seller Information.

Set up how to get paid

To set up your payment methods click on the **Get Paid** tab.

The first option you see is Direct Checkout. This option lets buyers pay for items through Etsy using their credit or debit cards. Etsy charges 25 cents per order, plus 3% of the order total for using this service.

If you are a new seller, Etsy makes your funds available to you within three days, or as soon as you ship the item, whichever comes first. After you have been selling for 90 days, you can withdraw funds the next business day.

You can add additional payment methods by checking the link under the direct checkout box.

Additional payment methods include PayPal, Money Order, Personal Check, and Other. Make it easy on yourself, just accept PayPal. That's how 99% of your buyers will pay. If you decide to accept checks or Money Orders, allow 7 to 10 days for them to clear the bank before you ship your customer's purchase.

Listing your first item

Now that your shop is set up, it's time to list your first item.

- **Who made it?** Choices are: I did, a member of my shop, or another company or person. Select the one that applies.
- **Categories**. Use the drop-down menu, and select the category that best describes your item.
- **Add variations**. Variations are differences in your product listings such as size, color, etc. When a buyer selects your item, they will be required to choose the variations they want.

Keep in mind; variations don't show up in search. If you want the size, color, etc. to be searchable, you should set up a separate listing.

- **Photos**. You can add up to five photos to your listing. Make sure they are good clear photos that show all the details of what you are selling. If you have fancy frill work or designs, include a few close-ups of it.

Invest in a light box so you can take well-lit, close-up photos. You can find them for $30 to $40 on eBay and Amazon. What a light box does is help to diffuse the light so you can take a good clear picture of your item. Most light boxes come with several backdrops in a variety of colors to bring out the contrast in your pictures.

- **Title**. The key to writing a good title is to understand your title is the search string for your listing. It is how people find your listing on Etsy.

Think about every feature your item has. What terms will buyers use to search for your item? How else will they search for it? What period is it from the renaissance, 70's, 90's punk? Pick out the most important terms you can think of and pack them into the title.

- **Description**. Tell people what your item is. How it was made? What makes your item special compared to everybody else's?

Give people a compelling reason to buy your item. Tell them what's in it for them. If it is hand stitched, tell people. Let people know how you made it, or what materials you used to make it.

The more detailed information you include, the better chance, you will have of selling it.

- **Shop section**. If you set up shop sections, which section do you want to include it in.
- **Recipient**. Identify likely buyers. Most times you will want to leave this one blank. The reason is you don't want to limit your chances to sell it by targeting just one type of buyer.

- **Occasion**. Will it be used for a special event? Like recipient, leave this one blank, unless you are sure it is for only one occasion such as a wedding or a prom.
- **Style**. Choose two styles that describe your item from the drop-down list.
- **Tags**. Just like your title, you want to load your tag section with keywords people will use to search for your item. Obvious keywords are the style, color, size, use, etc. Try to use as many phrases as possible that describe your item or what it is used for – prom dress, wedding dress, linen table cloth, or custom made lace and satin prom dress. Put yourself in your buyer's shoes for a minute. What words would you use to search for your item? Etsy gives you thirteen tags. Use every one of them.
- **Materials**. Some people want to know what materials you used to make your item. You can list up to thirteen separate materials.
- **Price**. Enter your price here.
- **Quantity**. How many of this item do you have for sale?
- **Shipping**. Be sure to state your processing time, and the country your item is shipping from.

In the ships to section, you can set your pricing. Set your price for domestic shipping first.

If you plan on shipping internationally, the first box will let you ship anywhere in the world and set a price for that. If you only want to ship to certain countries, you can choose them from the drop-down box, and price shipping to each country individually.

When you set a shipping price, make sure you include the cost of boxes, envelopes, bubble wrap, labels, tape, and driving to and from the post office. You don't want to set your price so high as to discourage people from buying from you, but you should try to cover all your costs.

Another option is to offer free shipping and roll the cost of shipping into the price of your item.

Whatever you do, keep your shipping costs competitive with other sellers offering similar items.

- **Preview** your item. If everything looks good, go ahead and press enter, to send your listing live.

That's it. You've listed your first item on Etsy. Once you have four or five listings under your belt, it will get quicker.

....

You now know how to set up your Etsy shop, list your items for sale, and how to discover items to sell and at what prices they are currently selling.

Get started today, and keep experimenting with new products and tweaking your Etsy shop. Success will follow your hard-work.

Sell it on Fiverr

Fiverr is a freelance marketplace where buyers and sellers can exchange cash for services. What's amazes me is every item featured on Fiverr is $5.00—almost.

There appears to be no limit to the types of services sellers can offer on Fiverr. Among the recent gigs (what Fiverr calls listings) are —

- Custom logo design
- Facebook header design
- Amazon book reviews and product reviews
- Puppet videos
- Kindle and eBook book covers
- Tarot readings
- Psychic readings
- Resume and cover letter writing
- Poetry Writing
- Business card design
- Infographic design

By now hopefully, you get the idea. If you can imagine it, you can find a way to offer it as a gig on Fiverr.

The very least you need to know

Fiverr is relatively new to the e-commerce scene.

Micha Kaufman and Shai Wininger founded the company in 2010. Every gig starts at $5.00, but that's changing as the site continues to reinvent itself. Sellers receive $4.00 for each completed gig. Fiverr's take is twenty percent or $1.00 from each five-dollar gig.

As of October 2016, there were over three million gigs listed on Fiverr.

Fiverr has a leveling system, like eBay's Top-Rated Seller Program.

- **Newbies** have limited options on Fiverr. They can offer two gig extras limited to $5.00, $10.00, and $20.00. New sellers are limited to accepting four gigs in one transaction.

- **Level One** status opens up more opportunities for sellers. To reach Level One status, sellers need to complete ten gigs in the previous thirty days with a minimum 90% satisfaction rating. After they level up, sellers can list up to 15 gigs at a time, offer "fast delivery" for extra profits, and provide custom orders up to $1500. Level One status also opens up another gig extra—for a total of three and allows sellers to accept eight orders in one transaction.

- **Level Two Sellers** are required to have completed 50 gigs in the last sixty days with a minimum 90% satisfaction rating. When they reach this level, sellers have the chance to increase their income significantly. Buyers can purchase up to twelve of their gigs at one time. Gig Extras jump to five, and the price range jumps to $5.00, $10.00, $20.00, and $40,00.

- Becoming a **Top-Rated Seller** is like receiving tenure at a major university. The process for reaching this status is somewhat mysterious. The Fiverr blog states the site editors "mutually" choose top Rated Sellers. What is clear though is once you receive this designation a whole new world of profit possibilities open up to you. Top-rated sellers can charge up to $100 for each gig extra, and they receive the Top-Rated Seller Badge next to each of their gigs.

If you are serious about making money on Fiverr, you need to level up as quickly as possible. The easiest way to do this is to offer a large selection of gigs and provide excellent customer service.

Gig Extras

Earlier I mentioned gig extras.

Gig extras are the method Fiverr has devised to let sellers take their income to the next level. To better understand how gig extras work, check out these extras offered by Professor Puppet.

Get more with my Gig Extras

- ☐ I will post your video on YouTube so you don't have to OR Deliver your video in 1080p HD PLEASE SPECIFY +$10
  Requires no additional time
- ☐ I will superimpose your URL or any message over your video Limit 2 supers per upgrade +$10
  Requires no additional time
- ☐ I will Shoot your video on my Green Screen and superimpose a different background +$50
  Requires no additional time
- ☐ I will RUSH SERVICE. I will drop everything and make your video FIRST before anything else in the queue +$20
  Requires no additional time

Even though every gig starts at $5.00, Professor Puppet can increase his take to $95.00 if someone adds all his gig extras to their order.

And, just in case you think most buyers stick with the basic $5.00 offer, think again! Professor Puppet has made two promotional videos for my businesses. Each time, I spent over $35.00.

So, if anyone out there is still wondering how you can make money selling each of your services for only five bucks, you know the answer – **GIG EXTRAS**. They can easily raise your average $5.00 sale to $25.00, or more.

One final thought on gig extras. The best gig extras don't necessarily have to cost you more time or money.

Most sellers offer very simple gig extras:

- Next day service for five, or ten dollars
- A PSD file of the graphic they already designed for an extra $5.00 to $20.00. It's no extra work – you already have it on your computer.
- Two extra revisions for $5.00, or $10.00.

- Your video delivered in additional formats for $10.00, or $20.00.
- A 3D cover to go with the 2D eBook cover they already designed for an additional $5.00.

The key to making the most money on Fiverr is to keep your gig extras simple and easy to perform, but still, make them appear valuable to your customers.

I saved the best part for last. Many sellers dangle a new-fangled cyber tip jar out there that lets them collect even more money.

Do you want to make even more money? The key is to give customers a compelling, or downright crazy reason to give you an extra-large tip.

One seller suggests an extra $5.00 would let him start his day with a latte from Starbucks, for $20.00 he could put a half a tank of gas in his old jalopy, and for $50.00 he would have a good start at taking his wife out for a romantic supper.

Who could resist giving this creative genius a tip?

Getting Started

Getting started as a seller on Fiverr is as easy as entering your email address and choosing a username and password. That's it, and you're a member of the Fiverr community.

Before you click the join button, take a few moments to think about your username. It is how people will come to know you on Fiverr.

A relevant username that complements the service you are providing will help to position you as an expert in the service you are offering.

Many people choose the first idea that pops into their head, or maybe their name. The thing is, if you name your business marysue or wonderwoman 113, people aren't going to have any idea what you do.

If you call yourself videoreviewer or bestlogodesigner, people are going to know right away what services you offer. A professional username can help position you as the right seller.

Seller Basics

Every gig on Fiverr starts with the words "I will ____ for ____."

As a seller, your job is to fill in the blanks. Just what is it you're willing to do for five bucks? Ten buck? Twenty buck? Or, whatever?

I know, some of you are saying – not much.

A recent Fiverr survey says there are thousands of sellers making $1000 to $2000, or more, every month selling their services on Fiverr. Some of the elite sellers make $5000 or more each, and every month.

So, before you turn your nose up at five bucks, let's examine some of the things you need to consider before creating your first gig.

Before you do anything, check the Fiverr website for two or three days. Explore categories, and click into as many gigs as you can.

Keep your pen and notebook handy. Whenever you see something you like or something, you think you might want to do – jot it down.

Write down the seller's username – the title of their gig – keywords they use to describe their gig – any special instructions they include in their descriptions. It's information you can use to craft your gigs.

Don't stop there. Check out the pictures, or samples they include. If the seller has a video describing the service they are offering, watch it, and make a few notes about what they say, and how they describe their gig.

Study the feedback left for gigs like yours. What did buyers like, or dislike, about them? Look for clues to help you design a better gig, and position yours, so more people will choose to do business with you.

You don't have to pick out your first gig right now, just get down as many ideas as you can.

Look over the gigs you examined.

Draw a star by the ones you think would be a good fit for you. Cross off the ones you don't think would be a good fit for you, or you can't see yourself doing.

This is where the rubber meets the road. At this point, you should have at least five gigs you think would give you a great start on Fiverr.

Make sure the gigs you choose are something you can make money doing.

Most sellers agree to make money you need to offer a service you can complete in no more than fifteen minutes. Five minutes or less is even better.

At fifteen minutes per gig, and an average profit of $4.00 per gig, that means you can make $16.00 per hour. If you can lower your working time to ten minutes per gig, you can make $24.00 per hour.

Now go back and evaluate the gig ideas you picked out. Be brutally honest.

Is this something you can do in fifteen minutes, or less? If not, is there a way you can do it faster? If not, scratch this gig off your list, or move it to your work on later pile.

Continue to evaluate each potential gig the same way.

If you're sure, you can complete them in fifteen minutes or less, great! Add them to your list of must do gigs.

The last step is to work a couple of your potential gigs to make sure how fast you can do them. Use a stopwatch to track your time. Make a list of your gigs by how much time they took you to complete.

Pick the gig you want to get started on today.

From here on out we are going to concentrate on getting this gig ready to post on Fiverr.

Create Your First Gig

Posting a gig on Fiverr consists of nine simple steps.

For this demonstration, we're going to assume you're going to sell a Kindle book cover. As we walk through the steps, take some time to reflect on each step, and how the process relates to creating your gig.

The gig shown below if from one of my favorite cover designers. Right now, she has 86 covers waiting in her queue over the next three days, so you know this lady is breaking her ass to get them done, but at the same time, she's making some serious bucks.

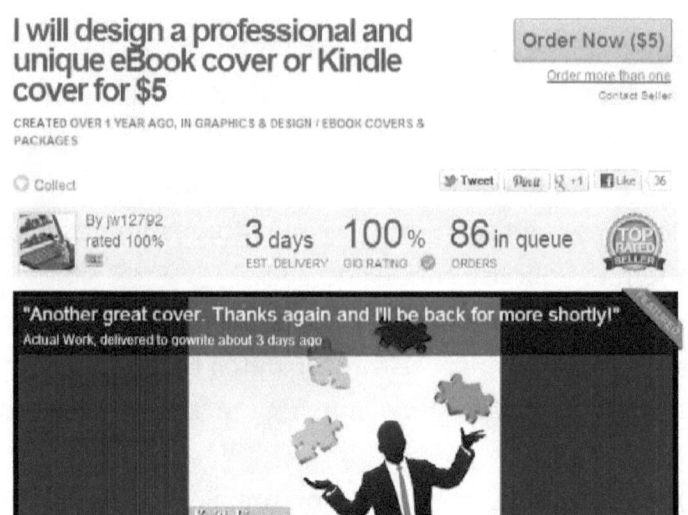

To get started, choose the Start Selling button at the top of Fiverr's main page.

Step 1. The first thing you're going to see are the familiar words, "I will _____ for $5.00."

Tell people what you're willing to do for $5.00. A good gig title should be short, tell people exactly what you are going to do for them, and be rich in keywords.

Look at the title for this gig. "I will design a professional and unique eBook cover or Kindle cover for $5.00."

It's a great title. It contains three main keywords "design," "eBook cover," and "Kindle cover." It also has two descriptors or adjectives "professional" and "unique."

The right keywords will give it a great shot at being picked up and shown by Fiverr's search engine every time someone searches for either "eBook cover" or "Kindle cover."

Step 2. Select a category. The beautiful thing here is Fiverr makes selecting a category super-easy. They only give you twelve choices: Fun & Bizarre, Online Marketing, Graphics and Design, Advertising, Writing & Translation, Lifestyle, Business, Programming & Tech, Other, Music & Audio, Gifts, and Video and Animation.

Choose the category that will give you the best bang for your buck.

Step 3. Description. Tell your story. Tell people what you are selling, what the benefits are for them, and what information you need from them to make it happen. If there are things you cannot, or will not do, this is the place to say it. A lot of sellers that offer art and writing services specify they won't write or draw pornography. Remember, it's your business, and what you choose to do, or not do, is up to you.

Let's look at the description in our sample listing.

*"Over 5,000 covers created to date! 3D Covers are FREE, and when I say three days, I mean three days – regardless of the orders in the queue...and I'm not happy until you are so UNLIMITED REVISIONS! Order now! * I also create covers for ALL genres, so let's hear what you have in mind. What makes my covers stand out from other designers here on Fiverr? I treat your cover as an individual! Are cars the theme of your book? How do metallic fonts and backgrounds sound? Chocolate the theme? We'll make book buyers want to lick the cover itself! Trust me; you'll love your cover. Order now!"*

What do you think?

This description offers so many examples of the things you should try to include in each, and every one of your gig descriptions. The seller tells you twice, to "Order Now!" She tells you once in the middle of the description, and again at the end.

She emphasizes her covers are different from those made by other designers on Fiverr. Then she tells you what makes them better and different – "We'll make book buyers want to lick the cover itself!"

She guarantees buyers will be pleased with their cover. "I'm not happy until you are so UNLIMITED REVISIONS!"

Take some time to read through the descriptions written by many different Top-Rated Sellers, and you will quickly learn the secrets to being more successful and selling more gigs on Fiverr.

Step 4. Instructions to Buyer. Tell buyers what information you need to put their gig together.

Fiverr uses this box to request information from buyers, so before you fill it out, take a few minutes to carefully decide what information you need to make the buyer's project come together. The clearer you are with your instructions, the easier it will be to complete your project in as little time as possible.

Another benefit will be better feedback because you completed your gig on time, and how the buyer wanted it.

Step 5. Tags. Tags are simply a list of keywords people use to search for your gig on Fiverr.

The easiest way to pick your tags is to see what keywords other sellers are using to tag their gigs. Choose the keywords you think are relevant, and add them here.

Step 6. Maximum days to complete. What's the longest it will take you to deliver the finished gig? As a new seller, you should strive to deliver every gig within twenty-four hours.

People like fast. Everybody wants to buy something today and get it yesterday. Many buyers will choose your gig over someone else's when you offer one day service, especially when other sellers list a three to five-day turnaround.

Only offer one-day turnaround if you can deliver on it. You will hurt your rankings and increase your chances of receiving negative feedback if you deliver late. If you're not sure you can deliver your gig in one day, decide how many days you think it will take you to complete your gig and then shoot to deliver as soon as you can. That will give buyers a pleasant surprise, and happy buyers mean good reviews.

Step 7. Add image. Upload images to illustrate your gig. These should be the best samples of your work. For illustrations, Fiverr recommends a .jpeg format, 600 pixels wide x 370 pixels high, with a maximum file size of 5 megabytes. Once you have your pictures ready, you can use MS Paint or another graphics program to resize them to 600 x 370 pixels.

It is also recommended you upload a video. It can be something as simple as you talking about how you produce your gigs, giving instructions on the information you need from the seller to bring their gig to life, or a collage showing your gigs and comments from the people who purchased them.

Keep it simple. Be informative. Better yet, make it humorous.

Step 8. This item requires shipping. If you are sending a physical product to buyers such as a small craft, check this box.

Step 9. Press the **Save** button.

Before you decide press save, take a few minutes to look it over first.

- Did you spell everything correctly?
- Did you include enough keywords in your title and description?
- Are your tags or keywords ones that buyers will use to search for your gig?
- Did you include all the information you're going to require in your information request line?

When you're happy with everything, press **Save** and your gig will go live.

Pretty simple, right?

Here are a few things you should keep in mind as you begin your career on Fiverr:

- Sellers can list a maximum of twenty gigs at one time. Choose the gigs you offer carefully. Make sure they are gigs you can complete the quickest, and that will sell the best.

- When you are first starting out, you're only allowed to offer two gig extras, but many sellers have found a clever way around this. They suggest buyers should purchase an additional gig if they want something extra. For example, if your gig is to write a 200-word SEO article for $5.00, you could mention that buyers "should purchase an extra gig for every additional 200 words." It gives you the same benefit as being able to offer a gig extra.

- Be careful about the types of gigs you offer. Reviews and testimonials are big business on Fiverr, but offering to write a bogus book or product reviews for Amazon items is against Amazon's terms of service. What you will discover is many of these reviewers have a very short lifespan on Fiverr, because they quickly get shut down.

- Always offer a great value for the money you are charging. It will come back to you in good reviews and more business over the long haul.

- Spend at least a half-hour every week checking through the gigs offered on Fiverr. Watch for new trends and services you may not currently be offering. It will help you to grow your business, and keep your offerings fresh and relevant.

Fiverr Selling 101

Fiverr continues to reinvent itself, as the freelance marketplace evolves. Gigs are no longer required to start at $5.00, but most buyers offer a $5.00 gig as a gateway to more expensive offerings.

We've already talked about gig extras. Depending upon your seller level they give you an amazing opportunity to boost your income while customizing your gigs to meet buyer wants and needs.

Package attributes is a relatively new feature that can boost your sales.

If you've spent any time on Fiverr, you probably know what I'm talking about—even if you don't recognize the name.

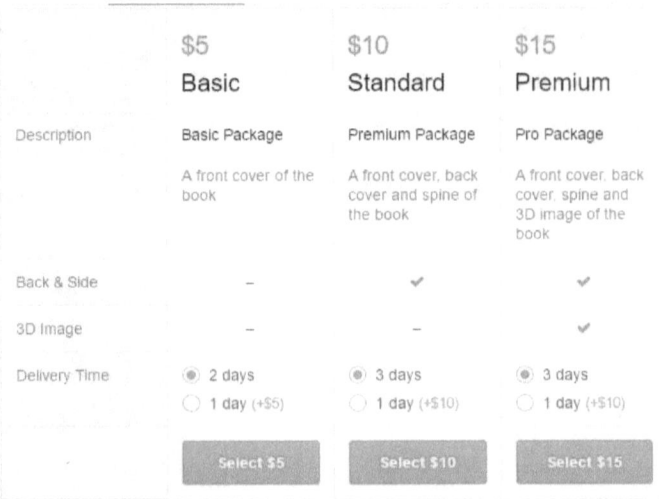

What I like about package attributes is they make it easy for buyers to compare your offerings. You can offer a basic product for $5.00, a step-up for $25.00, and a bigger step-up for $50.00. Most sellers are going to pick the middle option. They don't want to go to cheap, but they don't want to blow their whole wad either.

Package attributes make it easier to convert lookers into buyers because you're offering them more choices. I don't have any specific proof, but my guess is package attributes convert better than gig extras.

Experiment with your listings, and discover what works best for you.

Custom Offers are where the real money is at on Fiverr. Forbes Magazine did a story about four sellers who make $15,000 a month, or more, by using custom offers. One of the ladies profiled in the article runs an executive resume writing service. She went from making $5.00 per gig to making over $300,000 last year. A lot of her business comes from creating custom resume packages and selling them for $500 to $800 each—all by sending custom offers.

Think you can't do it? Think again.

Suppose you are a graphic designer who sells custom book covers on Fiverr. Create your listing just as you normally would. Add package attributes and gig extras to up-sell regular buyers. The only thing I want you to do differently is to add an additional line at the top and bottom of your item description page. It can be as simple as, "Are you looking for an eye-shattering design? Contact me for a *Custom Offer*."

That throws it back into the buyer's court. Some of them are going to be curious, and contact you. When they do, ask a few well-placed discovery questions, and fire off an offer to let them know what you can do for them.

Fiverr Anywhere works hand in hand with *Custom Offers* to help you make larger dollar sales.

Fiverr Anywhere started out as a Google Chrome extension. Since then it was moved to the Fiverr site. To access *Fiverr Anywhere* go to the Promote Your Business section under the My Sales Tab. Click on the Generate *Custom Offer* tab, then create your custom offer. After you've done that, you can retrieve your link. That will let you add your offer to your website, blog, email, or social media sites.

When someone contacts you, it works just like a regular *Custom Offer*. Potential buyers can accept your offer, or request a modification.

Use *Fiver Anywhere* and *Custom Offer* to grow your business and reach new buyers off the Fiverr website.

www.ingramcontent.com/pod-product-compliance
Lightning Source LLC
Chambersburg PA
CBHW021406170526
45164CB00002B/518